CONTENTS

Chapter 4

BETWEEN TWO BUNS: BURGER AND SANDWICH SAUCES | 75

Chapter 5

INTO THE SEA: SEAFOOD SAUCES | 101

Chapter 6

LIGHTER FARE: SALAD DRESSINGS AND MARINADES | 121

Chapter 9

~~DON'T~~ FILL UP ON DIP: HEARTY DIPS | 213

Chapter 10

DELICIOUS DIPPERS: DIPPABLE SIDES FOR PAIRING WITH SECRET SAUCES | 241

INTRODUCTION

Raising Cane's Cane's Sauce

Chipotle Guacamole

Whataburger Spicy Ketchup

For decades, restaurants have known the special power that sauces, dressings, and dips have to balance and elevate dishes—and for years, they've been able to keep those secrets to themselves. But now the secret is out with the help of *Secret Sauce*!

This book unlocks the mysteries behind crave-worthy sauces, dressings, and marinades so you can make them anytime without leaving your house, waiting in line, or spending your hard-earned money. Here you'll find two hundred recipes for some of the best-loved and most viral restaurant and fast-food sauces—and they all can be made at home for a fraction of the price most restaurants charge! From Chick-fil-A Sauce and Panera Bread Green Goddess Dressing to Taco Bell Mexican Pizza Sauce and McDonald's Big Mac Sauce, with *Secret Sauce* you will finally be able to re-create your favorite condiments at home.

You'll find recipes not just for sauces but for popular restaurant sides, breads, and dippers too. You'll also find a chapter with more hearty dips and spreads that can be eaten as appetizers or as part of a party spread. Additionally, there are tips for swaps and substitutions, history and fun facts about the sauces and restaurant chains, and ideas for different ways you can use the sauces. And don't worry about having to hunt for strange or unique ingredients to get those special flavors; all the recipes in this book use ingredients you can find at most grocery stores—and you'll discover that making these menu items at home is healthier than eating them at restaurants. There's also a chapter on the tools and ingredients you'll need to start making your sauces and some storage and safety tips so you can dip, spread, and dress your meals with confidence.

It's not a secret anymore: Now you can level up your sauce-making game with iconic restaurant copycat recipes that will give you and your guests a delicious reason to come back for more. Whether they're for dips, dressings, or delicious drizzles to finish your dish, *Secret Sauce* has the recipes you crave!

CHAPTER 1

SECRET SAUCES AT HOME

Have you ever tried to re-create a favorite secret sauce at home only to have the results fall flat? Were the flavors dull or the seasonings just not right? You are not alone! Restaurant chefs are constantly innovating and testing ingredients to develop tastier recipes in the hope of creating the next viral sensation. The good news is that you do not have to be a professional chef to re-create popular restaurant secret sauces at home. With the right recipes, tools, and techniques, you can wow your friends and family, and satisfy your own cravings, anytime you like and without having to spend an arm and a leg.

This chapter will provide you with the information you need to successfully re-create your favorite sauces at home. It breaks down the common ingredients used throughout the book as well as the tools and equipment you will need. There is also a section on preparation and tips on how to cook like a pro, how to present your creations for the best visual impact, and how to store your sauces for maximum freshness. Additionally, you will find tips for serving your sauces and guidance on food safety so every dip is fresh and flavorful.

A Brief History of the Secret Sauce

Secret or special sauces are alluring because they can transform ordinary foods into viral sensations and elevate them into cultural icons. While it is not really possible to pinpoint the exact origin of the term "secret sauce" or "special sauce," it seems the phrase "secret sauce" first appeared in 1906. "Special sauce" has been around a bit longer, with some references to it as far back as 1848. It started to gain popularity in the 1940s with restaurant menus highlighting their "special sauce" to attract customers. For example, an ad from 1949 for a Honolulu restaurant named Pier 40 Tavern referenced a "special sauce" on their De Luxe hamburger. A year earlier, In-N-Out Burger introduced their special burger sauce, called "spread," when they opened in 1948, and they claim their recipe remains unchanged to this day. Secret sauces truly burst onto the national scene with the introduction of McDonald's Big Mac in 1967. McDonald's Big Mac Sauce, the secret ingredient that made the burger different from other burgers on their menu, has since become one of the most beloved secret sauces of all time.

Modern marketing has leveraged the idea of a closely guarded "secret recipe" to attract customers, and this strategy has been wildly successful. In 1974, McDonald's released a jingle to market the Big Mac and its secret sauce that included the lyrics "Two all-beef patties, special sauce, lettuce, cheese, pickles, onions on a sesame seed bun." The jingle was a marketing success, with later ads featuring customers trying—and often hilariously failing—to sing the list of the burger's ingredients. Raising Cane's is a current example of a chain that has found tremendous social media success because of the viral popularity of their sauce. Influencers and mukbangers—people who eat large meals on camera—are frequently posting videos featuring a variety of foods dunked into extra-large drink cups filled with Cane's Sauce. Today, most restaurants claim to have at least one sauce or dressing they promote as their "secret sauce" to entice customers and gain attention on social media. It is common for fast-food chains to have multiple sauces for different menu items, including chicken nuggets, burgers, fries, fish, seafood, wings, and more.

Why are secret sauces so popular? People love a delicious mystery! What herbs and spices can you taste? What ingredients add that irresistible flavor? What makes the sauce so craveable? These sauces allow customers the freedom to use as much or as little as they wish and customize their meals to make them special. While it is easy to identify some secret ingredients—creamy sauces usually have mayonnaise, while tangy sauces have ketchup or barbecue sauce—other ingredients are harder to pinpoint. Also less obvious is what blend of sauces, herbs, and spices is used to achieve that craveable flavor. Too much of one ingredient or too little of another and you miss the unique flavor of the secret sauce entirely.

The Anatomy of a Secret Sauce

Secret sauces come in many varieties, from sauces slathered on burgers and sandwiches to sauces used for dipping and drizzling chicken, breadsticks, and more. What may surprise you is that most of these sauces simply are not all that special! They often use the same basic ingredients for their foundation. The unique flavors come from the different ratios of ingredients—such as mayonnaise, vinegar, hot sauce, and mustard—along with the different herbs and spices mixed in. This section breaks down a few of the most popular varieties of secret sauces and unveils the mysteries of how they are made.

Sandwich Sauces

The most popular burger sauces generally start with a creamy base, one of the most popular being a variation on Thousand Island dressing. This dressing, invented in the Thousand Islands area on the St. Lawrence River, is a mix of mayonnaise, tangy tomato, minced pickles, a touch of sugar, and various spices that can be customized to make the flavor unique. The savory-sweet flavor profile of the dressing makes it an excellent accompaniment to foods like burgers, vegetables, and fries. Restaurants will experiment with the different ingredients and even mix in other condiments like ranch or honey mustard to create a unique flavor people will associate with their chain. These sauces usually contain small chunks of pickle, onion, or other ingredients and have a rosy color. This category includes sauces like McDonald's Big Mac Sauce and In-N-Out Burger Animal Style Spread.

While Thousand Island–based dressings are widespread, some restaurants use a simple mayonnaise base that includes ingredients like ketchup, yellow mustard, honey mustard, or hot sauce mixed with a special blend of spices. Some, like Arby's with their Arby's Sauce, forgo the mayonnaise altogether to keep the sauce bright and tangy, which pairs well with cured or roasted meats. These sauces tend to be smooth or creamy, with some even doubling as a dipping sauce for fries, and they typically contain no discernable chunks.

Chicken Sauce

Chicken sauces generally fall into three categories: creamy, sweet and tangy, or vinegary and hot. Creamy chicken sauces are similar to burger spreads because of their mayonnaise base. Often you find other additions like ranch or honey mustard mixed into the base to brighten the flavor. Common additions to these sauces include honey, barbecue sauce, tomato paste, vinegar, or ketchup. These sauces often have spices like garlic, onion, pepper, and paprika added for extra flavor. Some sauces include a spicy kick from the addition of hot sauce or add some zing with a bit of pickle juice. In this category, you will find the viral Raising Cane's Cane's Sauce and KFC Sauce.

For sweet and tangy sauces, you'll often find a thick corn syrup or honey-based sauce similar in texture to Asian sweet and sour or Thai sweet chili sauce. Among the best known of these sauces are McDonald's Sweet 'N Sour Sauce, introduced in 1983, and Chick-fil-A Polynesian Sauce, added to the menu in 1984. These sauces often feature vinegar, tomato paste, ginger, and other flavors that balance out the sweet base. These sweet and tangy sauces offer a balance to the rich flavors of fried foods like chicken nuggets and tenders and roasted or grilled chicken.

The third common chicken sauce is wing sauce. Wings have become one of the fastest-growing items on restaurant menus, and their momentum shows no signs of slowing down. Buffalo wings have a bit of a murky history. However, the most popular story of their origin is that in 1964, Teressa Bellissimo created them at the Anchor Bar in Buffalo, New York, to feed a group of her son's friends. Today, wing sauces come in all sorts, with a range of flavors that can vary from vinegar and hot pepper based, to thick and creamy with Parmesan cheese and garlic, to sweet and tangy with a bold, spicy kick. Wing sauces are usually used for tossing fried chicken wings and boneless wings, but many restaurants will offer small cups of wing sauce for dunking tenders and nuggets or will toss breaded chicken fillets in wing sauce before using the chicken in a sandwich.

Fish and Seafood Sauces

Most people enjoy a good dipping sauce with seafood and fish dishes. Some are ubiquitous, such as lemon butter, tartar sauce, and cocktail sauce, and you will find most seafood restaurants have their own special recipe. Other seafood sauces are more specific to a cuisine or cultural food style. Cajun seafood boil sauces have become very popular on social media, and their butter base is mixed with seasonings such as lemon pepper, Cajun seasoning, or Old Bay. For fried or coconut shrimp, you will often see sauces made with a base of sweet coconut cream and flavored with fruit like pineapple or apricot for sweetness and tang, like in Red Lobster Piña Colada Sauce. In Asian cuisine, where you find bold, warm flavors, you will see sauces made with a soy sauce and vinegar base mixed with fresh ginger and garlic, and for a kick there can also be chili flakes. Some have a touch of toasted sesame oil for toasty richness.

Salad Dressings

Salad dressings have a long history, with records of oil and vinegar mixtures being used to flavor salads by the Babylonians about two thousand years ago. Today, salad dressings come in a full spectrum of flavors and textures, from simple vinaigrette dressings to more complex, creamy dressings with herbs, fruits, and cheeses.

Vinaigrettes are made with an oil and vinegar base, with other flavors added like herbs, spices, and sometimes cheese or fruit purée. Popular oils used in this variety of dressing include olive oil, vegetable oil, avocado oil, and sesame oil. For vinegars, you will often see balsamic, red wine, apple cider, and champagne used. Some popular examples of this type include Applebee's Neighborhood Grill + Bar Oriental Vinaigrette, Panera Bread Fuji Apple Vinaigrette, or On The Border Mexican Grill & Cantina Smoked Jalapeño Vinaigrette.

Creamy dressings are usually mayonnaise or dairy based and include herbs, spices, cheese, or other ingredients like salsa and citrus. Chick-fil-A Avocado Lime Ranch and Wendy's Ghost Pepper Ranch are among some of the better known of this type. In the United States, ranch dressing is wildly popular and is a common addition to secret sauces, and it is used as a base for salad dressings like Red Robin Salsa-Ranch Dressing.

Other Sauces, Salsas, and Condiments

This last category encompasses marinades, gravies, salsas, and sauces that don't quite fit the other previous categories. Think cheese sauces, finishing sauces, gravies, and dessert sauces. These sauces are specific in their uses—for example, sausage gravy for topping buttermilk biscuits or hot fudge sauce for drizzling over ice cream—but can still be iconic for their flavor and popularity. A couple of the most viral in this category include Taco Bell Nacho Cheese Sauce, which is used for dipping chips and their popular Nacho Fries, and Whataburger Spicy Ketchup, a condiment that became so popular when it was released as a limited-edition menu item in 2012 that it was added permanently in 2013.

Ingredients to Have On Hand

Fresh ingredients will always have the best flavor! While it is not practical to have every single ingredient on hand at all times, there are some common ingredients you will find throughout this book that you may want to consider having on hand if you love sauces, dips, and dressings. While not comprehensive, the following lists will give you a solid base of flavors to work with when making your favorite sauce recipes.

Dry Ingredients

This section lists dry ingredients, including baking staples and herbs and spices, that you will see frequently throughout this book. If you like, you can purchase the freeze-dried versions of the herbs listed for better flavor.

- All-purpose flour
- Cayenne pepper
- Chili powder
- Cloves, ground and whole
- Cornstarch
- Dried basil
- Dried chives
- Dried dill
- Dried oregano
- Dried parsley
- Dried thyme
- Garlic powder
- Ground cinnamon
- Ground cumin
- Ground nutmeg
- Onion powder
- Paprika
- Sesame seeds
- Smoked paprika

Bottled, Canned, and Jarred Ingredients

The items in this section are some common bases and flavor enhancers in many of the most popular secret sauces and dips. This list provides a solid starting point for a variety of recipes in this book.

- Barbecue sauce
- Chipotle peppers in adobo
- Coco Lopez Cream of Coconut
- Green chilies, diced
- Honey
- Hot pepper sauce
- Ketchup
- Mayonnaise
- Mustard, yellow and Dijon
- Olive oil
- Pickle relish, sweet and dill
- Prepared horseradish
- Soy sauce
- Teriyaki sauce
- Thai sweet chili sauce
- Vinegar (red, rice, and balsamic)
- Worcestershire sauce

Refrigerated and Fresh Ingredients

Fresh ingredients should always be kept refrigerated until ready to use.

- Butter or margarine
- Block cheeses (Cheddar, Monterey jack, Swiss, Parmesan, sliced American, and so on)
- Cream cheese
- Eggs, large
- Fruit (strawberries, blueberries, lemons, limes, oranges, and so on)
- Heavy cream
- Milk (whole)
- Ricotta cheese
- Sour cream
- Vegetables (cucumbers, garlic, jalapeños, onions, tomatoes, and so on)

Tools and Appliances

Cooking is more fun when you have the right tools, and this section will outline what you need to whip up your favorite secret sauces like a pro! You don't need a professional kitchen to get professional results. Just a few everyday tools and appliances will have you set for success. As you read, you will find information on tools and equipment that will make preparing the recipes in this book a cinch and help you unlock your inner chef!

Hand Tools

Following is a list of hand tools and supplies needed for most of the recipes in this book. The good news is that making secret sauces, dips, and dressings does not require more than a few tools you may already have on hand.

- 8-inch nonstick skillet
- 10-inch nonstick skillet
- Baking sheets
- Bottle opener
- Box grater
- Can opener
- Chef's knife
- Colander
- Cutting board
- Microplane zester
- Paring knife
- Saucepans with lids (1-quart and 2-quart)
- Set of measuring cups
- Set of measuring spoons
- Set of mixing bowls
- Set of storage containers with airtight lids
- Silicone whisk
- Spatulas, large and small
- Whisk, balloon or French, small

Appliances

Appliances help you prepare and cook with greater ease and speed. Stand and hand mixers, for example, take a lot of the strain out of cooking. The list that follows includes the appliances you will use most often while cooking from this book.

- Blender
- Electric deep fryer or deep-sided Dutch oven
- Food processor
- Handheld mixer or stand mixer
- Instant-read thermometer
- Microwave oven
- Oven or toaster oven
- Refrigerator
- Stove, electric or gas

Preparation and Serving

A little preparation goes a long way in the kitchen and is the key to that professional polish. Taking the time to prepare will mean you will not have any kitchen catastrophes. Nothing feels worse than not having a key ingredient when you need it, discovering you don't have adequate time to prepare the recipe, or struggling because you do not have the right tools. This section offers tips and guidance to make cooking not just easier but a total blast!

Read the Recipe

The first, and most important, step to culinary success when cooking is to read your recipe from start to finish. Make note of divided ingredients and when they are used, oven preheating instructions, pan size and preparation instructions, and mention of tools you will need. Look out for any instructions for resting or chilling that may be required during or at the end of the recipe, as they usually guarantee the best flavor and texture.

Gather Tools

Next, gather your tools. Restaurant kitchens are usually well organized and will have the ingredients prepped and ready for cooking. You should apply this to your home kitchen too! Work in a comfortable space large enough to move around. Gather what you need, including measuring cups and spoons; hand tools like whisks, spatulas, or mixers; bowls; cutting boards; and serving or storage containers for the finished product. This will make your kitchen a frustration-free zone since you will not need to scramble to find what you need while you are working.

Gather and Prepare Ingredients

Having your ingredients prepped and ready is a top restaurant cooking tip. Round up all the ingredients you will need and have them ready before you get started. Be sure that you have enough of each ingredient and that none has spoiled or exceeded an expiration date. Nobody wants the interruption of an emergency grocery run! Checking expiration dates is a good habit to get into for fresh and refrigerated foods—fresh food tastes better. If there are any special preparation instructions, such as chopping vegetables, toasting nuts, or straining canned or jarred items, see to them before you start cooking.

Taste and Adjust

Good chefs take the time to taste as they go. This is their moment to tweak the flavors until things are seasoned just right. Take a little taste of your dips, dressings, marinades, and sauces after they are mixed to make sure they have the right balance of flavors and are seasoned to your preference. If something tastes a bit flat to you, you can add some extra herbs, spices, and salt or use a tried-and-true restaurant secret and add a squeeze of lemon or lime juice. A little bit of acid can take a dull dish and make it shine. For baked dips or recipes that require cooking before serving, heat a small amount in a skillet so it is safe to taste. It is difficult to add seasoning after cooking, so try this easy trick for testing seasoning.

Serve

The recipe is ready! You can choose to serve dips and sauces family style so your guests can help themselves. If you are plating the food, consider doing what restaurants do and adding an individual serving-sized cup of dip to each plate. No matter how you choose to present your sauces or dips, a little garnish—some finely chopped parsley or a dash of paprika—adds to their aesthetic appeal. For heartier appetizer-style baked dips, be sure you have an oven safe pan that can also be used for serving, and use a damp towel to quickly wipe down any messy edges for that perfect, clean look. Storing salad dressings in a glass bottle with a tight-fitting lid makes storage and serving a breeze. For burger and sandwich sauces, a plastic squeeze bottle is often a good choice for mess-free serving, and you can use these bottles to make fun designs—like smiley faces—for younger guests!

Storage and Safety

You have taken the time to whip up a batch of a secret sauce. What is the best way to ensure it stays fresh? This section will provide you with tips for storage and safety so you can rest assured that you know your sauce is good to go when a craving calls!

Starting with Fresh Ingredients

When building a sauce, be sure your ingredients are fresh and not expired. Check the expiration or best-by date for each ingredient, then take a moment to sniff and taste your ingredients to make sure they are fresh and flavorful. Starting with fresh ingredients will lead to a fresher, tastier result.

Safe Food Handling

Before you start cooking, clean the work area you plan to use with a disinfectant cleaner. Be sure your tools and bowls are clean, and wash your hands well with soap and warm water. Make sure to keep perishable ingredients refrigerated until you need them—or as specified by the recipe.

Safe Storage

Prepared sauces should be refrigerated below 40°F after mixing and until ready to serve. Store prepared sauces and dressings in airtight containers or bottles (including squeeze bottles) with tight-fitting caps. Prepared foods that are ready to eat should be cooked and stored at or below 40°F within 2 hours. Remember, foods having an internal temperature of 40°F–140°F for 2 hours or longer are in danger of causing foodborne illness. Be sure to store raw foods separately from fresh or ready-to-eat foods, with raw foods stored on lower shelves from cooked foods.

CHAPTER 2

TURN UP THE HEAT: SPICY SAUCES AND SALSAS

People love spicy foods, hot sauces, and salsas, and it's not hard to see why. Hot sauces and salsas can take a bland meal and make it exciting. Be it a zingy salsa to serve with warm tortilla chips as an appetizer, a bit of spicy ketchup to accompany your French fries, or a spicy, creamy sauce to drizzle over your main dish, a hot sauce or salsa can add some zest and heat to an everyday meal. This chapter has recipes for some of the most popular restaurant salsas and hot sauces so you can enjoy them anytime. No matter what kind of spicy sauces you like, this chapter has you covered! There are tomato-based salsas like Chili's famous Fresh Salsa and Abuelo's Mexican Restaurant Salsa Especial, creamy sauces like Taco Bell Creamy Jalapeño Sauce and Nando's PERi Ranch, plus fresh and chunky salsas like Moe's Southwest Grill Pico de Gallo and Bahama Breeze Pineapple-Mango Salsa. This chapter has recipes for the spicy sauces you crave. So, turn up the heat and add some spice to your life with zesty, tangy, and tasty spicy sauces and salsas!

ABUELO'S MEXICAN RESTAURANT SALSA ESPECIAL

Typically Served With: Tortilla Chips

Abuelo's Mexican Restaurant was founded in 1989 in Amarillo, Texas, as an upscale Mexican dining experience. This popular, medium-spicy tomato-based salsa is part of the trio of salsas offered to guests with warm tortilla chips for dipping. It has a bright, fresh flavor from the cilantro, lime juice, and onion that is balanced by the rich, charred flavor from the pan-roasted jalapeño and garlic. Whole, peeled canned tomatoes give this salsa the right texture to cling well to chips and stay chunky after being pulsed in the food processor.

YIELDS 2 CUPS, 1/4 CUP PER SERVING

2 medium jalapeños, sliced in half, stems and seeds removed
2 cloves garlic, peeled and left whole
1 (14-ounce) can whole peeled tomatoes, drained, juices reserved
3 tablespoons finely minced sweet onion
3 tablespoons finely chopped fresh cilantro leaves
1 tablespoon fresh lime juice
1/4 teaspoon salt

1. In an 8-inch nonstick skillet over medium heat, add jalapeños and garlic and cook, turning often, until softened and lightly charred, 8–10 minutes.
2. Transfer jalapeños and garlic to a food processor along with tomatoes and pulse until coarsely chopped, 10–12 pulses.
3. Transfer mixture to a glass jar with a tight-fitting lid and stir in remaining ingredients. If mixture is too thick, add reserved tomato juice a tablespoon at a time until desired consistency is reached. Refrigerate at least 4 hours before serving. Store up to 1 week in the refrigerator.

ABUELO'S MEXICAN RESTAURANT SALSA TROPICAL

Typically Served With: Tortilla Chips

This fresh tomatillo-based salsa is popular for its freshness with a hint of tropical sweetness from pineapple and fresh lime juice. It is a part of the salsa trio that is enjoyed by guests upon being seated. You can easily adjust the kick to your liking by adding more or less jalapeño, but using more than three can impact the final flavor. Tomatillos have both a husk and a sticky coating to deter insects. Take the time to thoroughly peel and wash the sticky residue off the tomatillos with warm water before use.

YIELDS 2 CUPS, 1/4 CUP PER SERVING

6 large tomatillos, husks removed and washed
1 medium jalapeño, stem and seeds removed
1 small sweet onion, peeled and cut into 1-inch pieces
1 clove garlic, peeled and smashed
1/4 cup loosely packed fresh cilantro leaves
1/4 cup drained canned pineapple chunks
1 tablespoon fresh lime juice
1/2 teaspoon granulated sugar
1/4 teaspoon salt

1. Quarter tomatillos and add to a food processor along with jalapeño, onion, garlic, and cilantro. Pulse 6–8 times until salsa is very chunky. Add remaining ingredients and pulse 3–5 times until salsa is well mixed and no large chunks remain.
2. Transfer salsa to a glass jar with a tight-fitting lid and refrigerate at least 4 hours before serving. Store up to 4 days in the refrigerator.

Made from Scratch

Abuelo's prides themselves on cooking with fresh ingredients, providing superior hospitality, giving guests an affordable yet upscale dining experience, and serving delicious freshly made food inspired by family recipes from Chef Luis E. Sanchez. They make their tortillas, side dishes, enchiladas, and salsas in-house, and that fresh-from-scratch flavor keeps people coming back!

BAHAMA BREEZE PINEAPPLE-MANGO SALSA

Typically Served With: Tequila Sunburn Glazed Salmon

Bahama Breeze is an American restaurant chain founded in Orlando, Florida, in 1996 and is known for its tropical, Caribbean-inspired menu that features bright flavors and fresh ingredients. This salsa is commonly served as a topping for Tequila Sunburn Glazed Salmon and is used as a garnish for other dishes. It is just the right mix of sweet, savory, and fresh with a chunky texture! Enjoy this as a topping for seafood tacos or fried or grilled fish or shrimp, or as a garnish for a crisp green salad.

YIELDS 2 CUPS, 1/4 CUP PER SERVING

1 medium mango, peeled, seeded, and finely chopped
1 cup finely diced fresh pineapple
2 medium jalapeños, stems and seeds removed, finely chopped
1 small red bell pepper, stem and seeds removed, finely chopped
1/2 small red onion, peeled and finely chopped
1/3 cup loosely packed fresh cilantro leaves, finely chopped
1/4 cup fresh lime juice
1/4 teaspoon salt
1/4 teaspoon ground black pepper

1. Place all ingredients in a medium bowl and mix well to combine.
2. Transfer salsa to an airtight container and refrigerate at least 4 hours before serving. Store up to 4 days in the refrigerator.

Caribbean Jerk Grilled Snapper

Looking for the perfect fish dish to serve with this salsa? Season 1 pound red snapper fillets with 1 teaspoon Caribbean jerk seasoning. In a grill pan over medium heat, add 1 teaspoon vegetable oil and brush to coat pan. Add fish and cook 2–3 minutes per side until fish flakes easily. Serve with salsa for garnish.

CHILI'S FRESH SALSA

Typically Served With: Dip Trio

Chili's Fresh Salsa is made using a seasoned, cooked tomato base with fresh crushed tomatoes added in at the restaurant the day of serving. This salsa has a smooth texture, and it pairs well with Chili's extra-thin corn tortilla chips fried fresh in-house daily. The salsa has been featured on the menu since 1975, the year the first Chili's restaurant opened in Dallas, Texas, by Larry Lavine. You can order this salsa as an appetizer, but it is also served when you order Chili's Skillet Beef Queso (Chapter 9).

YIELDS 2 CUPS, 1/4 CUP PER SERVING

2 medium Roma tomatoes
2 whole canned jalapeños, stems removed, chopped
1 clove garlic, peeled and crushed
1 (14-ounce) can crushed tomatoes
1/4 cup minced sweet onion
1 tablespoon fresh lime juice
1/2 teaspoon ground cumin
1/4 teaspoon salt

1. In a 1-quart saucepan, add 3 cups water. Bring to a boil over medium-high heat. Cut a small "x" into the bottom of each tomato with a paring knife and add to boiling water. Cook 1 minute, then transfer to a large bowl of ice water and let cool 3 minutes. Peel away skin, then cut and remove stems and seeds.
2. Transfer blanched tomatoes, jalapeños, and garlic to a food processor and pulse 10 times or until tomatoes and jalapeños are chunky. Add remaining ingredients and pulse 10–12 times until salsa is desired consistency.
3. Transfer mixture to glass jar with a tight-fitting lid and refrigerate at least 4 hours before serving. Store up to 4 days in the refrigerator.

CHILI'S NASHVILLE HOT SAUCE

Typically Served With: Nashville Hot Chicken Crispers

Nashville hot sauce is a bold, red hot sauce created by African American chefs as early as the 1930s in Nashville, Tennessee. It is most commonly used for coating fried chicken, and the flavors can vary from mild to very spicy. Over the last 20 years, the popularity of the sauce has skyrocketed in the US. In 2023, Chili's jumped on the trend and introduced their Nashville Hot Sauce to coat their fried Chicken Crispers and wings. The sauce was a hit, and today it is also used to coat their viral Fried Mozzarella (Chapter 10).

YIELDS 1 CUP, 2 TABLESPOONS PER SERVING

½ cup ghee
¼ cup cayenne pepper
2 tablespoons packed light brown sugar
1 tablespoon paprika
¼ teaspoon garlic powder
¼ teaspoon onion powder

In a 1-quart saucepan over medium heat, add ghee. Once ghee is melted, after about 3 minutes, add remaining ingredients and whisk until smooth. Continue to cook 3 minutes, making sure the sauce does not start to bubble. Remove from heat and cool 2 minutes before serving.

Add a Chili's Presidente Margarita

What goes better with spicy food than a margarita? In a chilled, salt-rimmed rocks glass, combine 1¼ ounces Sauza Commemorativo Añejo Tequila, ½ ounce Presidente brandy, ½ ounce Cointreau, 4 ounces sour mix, and 1 teaspoon fresh lime juice. Once combined, add additional ice and serve.

CHIPOTLE FRESH TOMATO SALSA

Typically Served With: Burrito

This mild salsa, inspired by traditional pico de gallo, was one of the original salsas offered when Chipotle first opened their doors in 1993. It is a chunky fresh salsa made from tomato, onion, chili peppers, lime, salt, and cilantro. The bright flavors are perfect as an addition to a burrito, burrito bowl, or tacos, but you can also enjoy this with freshly made Chipotle Chips (Chapter 10). This salsa tastes best when you use the ripest tomatoes available, so feel free to swap Roma tomatoes for the best quality of a tomato variety you can find.

YIELDS 2 CUPS, 1/4 CUP PER SERVING

1 pound Roma tomatoes, stems and seeds removed, chopped
2 large jalapeños, stems and seeds removed, finely chopped
1/4 cup finely chopped red onion
1/4 cup roughly chopped cilantro leaves
3 tablespoons freshly squeezed lime juice
1/2 teaspoon sea salt

In a medium bowl, combine tomatoes, jalapeños, onion, and cilantro. Mix well. Add lime juice and salt and toss to coat. Transfer to a glass jar with a tight-fitting lid and refrigerate 4 hours before serving. Store up to 4 days in the refrigerator.

Commitment to Freshness

Chipotle was inspired by the burrito stands of San Francisco, and they pride themselves on their use of fresh, simple ingredients. They claim they use just fifty-three ingredients on their entire menu! Their website lists the ingredients, and when you select one, it shows you the recipes that include it.

CHIPOTLE ROASTED CHILI-CORN SALSA

Typically Served With: Burrito

Sweet, smoky, and fresh, this salsa adds a refreshing flavor that pairs well with spiced meats and beans. This salsa can be enjoyed year-round by using frozen corn kernels, but if fresh corn is in season, feel free to swap fresh for frozen. To use fresh corn: Remove the husks and the silk. Then cut kernels from the cob until you have 16 ounces—roughly four cobs. In a 10-inch skillet over medium heat, add 1 tablespoon vegetable oil and once hot, add corn and sauté 6–8 minutes. Cook and continue as directed in step 4.

YIELDS 3 CUPS, 1/4 CUP PER SERVING

1 medium poblano pepper
16 ounces frozen corn kernels
1 tablespoon water
1/4 cup finely diced red onion
1/4 cup finely chopped cilantro leaves
1 1/2 large jalapeños, stems and seeds removed, finely chopped
2 teaspoons freshly squeezed lemon juice
2 teaspoons freshly squeezed lime juice
1/4 teaspoon sea salt

1. Preheat broiler to 500°F and line a baking sheet with aluminum foil.
2. Place poblano pepper on prepared baking sheet and broil 3–5 minutes per side until pepper is charred and tender on all sides. Transfer pepper to a medium bowl with a lid. Cover and let cool 15 minutes.
3. Once cooled, peel charred flesh off pepper but do not rinse. You want some small charred bits. Slice pepper in half and remove stem and seeds, then chop. Set aside.
4. In a 10-inch nonstick skillet over medium heat, add corn and water. Cover skillet, then reduce heat to medium-low and cook 3–5 minutes, stirring occasionally, until corn is warm and tender. Remove pan from heat and let corn cool.
5. In a medium bowl, combine poblano pepper, corn, and remaining ingredients. Toss to coat well. Serve immediately. Store up to 4 days in the refrigerator.

CHIPOTLE ROASTED CHILI-CORN SALSA

CHIPOTLE TOMATILLO–GREEN CHILI SALSA

Typically Served With: Burrito

Looking for a bit of heat and a zingy, roasted tomatillo flavor to add to your favorite Mexican dishes? This medium-heat salsa is just what you are looking for! This salsa is roasted to soften and lightly char the vegetables while releasing their flavors, then it is puréed in a blender until smooth. If you prefer a chunky salsa, you can pulse the ingredients in a food processor or in the blender until your preferred texture is reached. For more heat, add one small stemmed and seeded fresh jalapeño to the blender before puréeing.

YIELDS 2 CUPS, 1/4 CUP PER SERVING

1 pound tomatillos, husks removed and washed
2 Roma tomatoes, stems and seeds removed
1 large jalapeño, stem removed, cut in half
2 cups water
1 (4-ounce) can diced green chilies
1/2 cup packed fresh cilantro leaves
1 tablespoon freshly squeezed lime juice
1 teaspoon dried Mexican oregano
1 teaspoon ground cumin
1/2 teaspoon sea salt

1. Preheat oven to 450°F and line a baking sheet with aluminum foil. Lightly coat foil with nonstick cooking spray. Set aside.
2. Slice tomatillos in half and place cut side down on prepared baking sheet along with tomatoes and jalapeño. Roast 20–25 minutes until vegetables are lightly charred and tender. Remove from oven and cool 10 minutes.
3. Transfer roasted vegetables to a blender along with remaining ingredients. Purée until smooth, 15–20 seconds.
4. Transfer to a jar with an airtight lid and refrigerate 4 hours before serving. Store up to 7 days in the refrigerator.

DAIRY QUEEN FLAMETHROWER SAUCE

Typically Served With: FlameThrower Signature Stackburger

Dairy Queen FlameThrower Sauce is available at most Dairy Queen locations in the US and Canada (except in Texas—more on that in the sidebar). It is a creamy flavor bomb designed to enhance the meaty flavors of the burgers it is added to. The sauce is a well-balanced mixture of sweet, spicy, and smoky, with some savory spices to round out the flavor.

YIELDS 2/3 CUP, 2 TABLESPOONS PER SERVING

1/2 cup mayonnaise
3 tablespoons red pepper hot sauce, such as Tabasco
2 teaspoons chipotle pepper in adobo, mashed into a paste
1 1/2 teaspoons granulated sugar
1/2 teaspoon paprika
1/4 teaspoon mustard powder
1/4 teaspoon garlic powder
1/4 teaspoon onion powder
1/4 teaspoon white vinegar

Combine all ingredients in a small bowl. Whisk to combine. Cover and refrigerate 4 hours before serving. Store up to 10 days in the refrigerator.

Dairy Queen in Texas

Rolly Klose opened the first Texas Dairy Queen franchise in Austin in 1947 and is responsible for the menu quirks that exist in Texas today. These menu quirks include things like Hungr-Buster burgers, Tex-Mex offerings like tacos, and chicken fried steak finger baskets and sandwiches. They also have a special jingle, "DQ, that's what I like about Texas"!

DEL TACO CHIPOTLE SAUCE

Typically Served With: Chipotle Crispy Chicken Taco

In 1964 in Yermo, California, Ed Hackbarth and David Jameson opened the first Del Taco, and today the chain has almost six hundred locations in seventeen states. Del Taco Chipotle Sauce is featured on menu items such as the Chipotle Crispy Chicken Taco and the Epic Carne Asada Steak Cali Bacon Burrito. It is a creamy blend of chipotle, spices, and a mix of mayonnaise and ranch dressing for a savory kick. Be sure to scrape down the sides of the blender a few times to make this sauce smooth and creamy.

YIELDS 1 CUP, 2 TABLESPOONS PER SERVING

½ cup mayonnaise
3 tablespoons prepared buttermilk ranch dressing
2 tablespoons chopped chipotle in adobo
½ teaspoon lime juice
¼ teaspoon chili powder
¼ teaspoon paprika
¼ teaspoon ground cumin

1. Place all ingredients in a blender. Purée until smooth, scraping down sides of blender as needed.
2. Transfer to an airtight container and refrigerate 4 hours before serving. Store up to 7 days in the refrigerator.

DEL TACO CHIPOTLE SAUCE

MOE'S SOUTHWEST GRILL PICO DE GALLO

Typically Served With: Moe Meat Moe Cheese Burrito

What makes this unconventional version of the traditional Mexican fresh salsa different from other recipes? It's the Southwest-inspired seasonings added to the fresh ingredients for a rich earthy flavor. Along with the seasonings, this pico de gallo has plenty of fresh tomato and fresh lime juice to keep the flavors bright. You can use 2 teaspoons of a favorite Southwest seasoning spice blend you might have on hand in place of the spices and herbs listed in this recipe, starting with the chili powder. Make this recipe for your next Taco Tuesday, and everyone will be saying, "Welcome to Moe's!"

YIELDS 2½ CUPS, ¼ CUP PER SERVING

6 medium Roma tomatoes, stems and seeds removed, chopped
1 cup loosely packed cilantro leaves, finely chopped
½ white onion, peeled and finely chopped
1 large jalapeño, stem and seeds removed, finely chopped
2 tablespoons freshly squeezed lime juice
½ teaspoon sea salt
½ teaspoon chili powder
¼ teaspoon ground cumin
¼ teaspoon garlic powder
¼ teaspoon Mexican oregano
¼ teaspoon smoked paprika
⅛ teaspoon onion powder

Combine all ingredients in a medium bowl and fold well to combine and evenly distribute seasonings. Cover and refrigerate 2 hours before serving. Store up to 3 days in the refrigerator.

Welcome to Moe's!

When you enter a Moe's Southwest Grill, the first thing you will hear is their staff shouting their iconic greeting, "Welcome to Moe's!" They claim it shows their customers that from the moment they walk in, they are welcome and in for a fun and delicious meal.

NANDO'S PERI-PERI SAUCE

Typically Served With: PERi-PERi Chicken

You can adjust the heat of this sauce by adding or reducing the number of bird's eye chilies used. For an extra-hot sauce, use as many as ten chilies. For a milder sauce, use two or three chilies. If you use fewer chilies, add one additional roasted red bell pepper to ensure the flavor and consistency is unchanged. You can use this sauce as a marinade or as a finishing sauce on the grill. One batch of sauce is enough to marinate one whole 5-pound chicken or four leg and thigh quarters.

YIELDS 1 CUP, 2 TABLESPOONS PER SERVING

3 tablespoons white vinegar
6 fresh bird's eye chilies, stems removed
2 roasted red bell peppers from a jar, drained and patted dry
1 teaspoon freshly squeezed lemon juice
1 teaspoon fresh lemon zest
1/4 cup chopped white onion
1 tablespoon chili powder
2 cloves garlic, peeled
1 dried bay leaf
1/2 teaspoon paprika
1/4 teaspoon salt
1/8 teaspoon allspice
3 tablespoons vegetable oil

1. In a blender, add all ingredients except oil and purée on high until smooth, about 30–40 seconds.
2. With the blender running, slowly drizzle in oil. Use immediately or transfer to a glass jar with a tight-fitting lid and refrigerate up to 4 days. Shake well before use.

NANDO'S PERI RANCH

Typically Served With: PERi-PERi Wings

Nando's is a South African restaurant chain founded in 1987 in Johannesburg, featuring Portuguese-style grilled chicken flavored with Mozambican flavors that include fiery African bird's eye—or peri-peri—chili. The chain has 1,200 locations in thirty countries. Their first restaurant in the US opened in Washington, DC, in 2008, and they have since expanded to almost fifty locations across the US. Their primary menu offering is grilled chicken both on the bone and boneless, but they also have other dishes like hummus, salads, chips (aka French fries), sandwiches, garlic bread, and wraps.

YIELDS 1½ CUPS, 2 TABLESPOONS PER SERVING

½ cup Nando's PERi-PERi Sauce, prepared (see recipe in this chapter)
½ cup mayonnaise
½ cup low-fat buttermilk
½ teaspoon onion powder
½ teaspoon dried dill
¼ teaspoon ground black pepper
¼ teaspoon garlic powder
¼ teaspoon sea salt

In a medium bowl, combine all ingredients and whisk until smooth. Transfer to a glass jar with a tight-fitting lid. Refrigerate 6 hours or overnight. Store up to 7 days in the refrigerator.

P.F. CHANG'S SIGNATURE SPICY DIPPING SAUCE

Typically Served With: Crispy Green Beans

If you have ever enjoyed the tempura-battered Crispy Green Beans at P.F. Chang's, then you are familiar with the spicy, creamy dipping sauce served with it. The secret to this sauce is in the mayonnaise. P.F. Chang's uses Japanese-style mayonnaise with a richer egg flavor because it is made with egg yolks and milder rice vinegar as opposed to the whole eggs and white vinegar used in Western mayonnaise. If you want the sauce to have a bolder red color, feel free to mix in 1/4 teaspoon of paprika.

YIELDS 3/4 CUP, 2 TABLESPOONS PER SERVING

1/2 cup Japanese-style mayonnaise, such as Kewpie
1/4 cup sriracha
1 scallion, green part only, finely chopped
1/2 teaspoon rice vinegar
1/2 teaspoon garlic paste

Mix all ingredients in a small bowl until well combined. Cover and refrigerate at least 4 hours before serving. Store up to 3 days in the refrigerator.

Dipper Ideas

This creamy sauce is excellent for dipping tempura vegetables, including green beans. You can follow the directions on Kikkoman Tempura Batter Mix for an easy and delicious tempura mix. Also consider this sauce for fried or grilled shrimp, pan-fried scallops, onion rings, and fresh vegetables like baby carrots, broccoli, and cauliflower florets.

TACO BELL AVOCADO RANCH SAUCE

Typically Served As: General Dipping Sauce

Taco Bell playfully asks on their website if their Avocado Ranch Sauce is a topping or a dip. The answer: It can be both—it is good on everything! This sauce is available to be swapped for the sauces offered on menu items, and it can also be ordered separately to be drizzled on nachos or tacos or as a dunk for burritos and Crunchwrap Supremes. While fresh avocado will give the best flavor in this sauce, you can use bagged mashed plain avocado in a pinch.

YIELDS 1⅓ CUPS, 2 TABLESPOONS PER SERVING

½ cup mayonnaise
½ cup low-fat buttermilk
⅓ cup cubed avocado
1 teaspoon lemon juice
½ teaspoon onion powder
½ teaspoon dried dill
¼ teaspoon ground black pepper
¼ teaspoon garlic powder
¼ teaspoon sea salt
⅛ teaspoon paprika

Combine all ingredients in a blender. Purée on high until smooth, about 30 seconds. Cover and refrigerate until ready to use. Store up to 4 days in the refrigerator.

The Liberty Bell Sale

In 1996, Taco Bell pulled a national April Fool's Day prank by claiming they were buying the Liberty Bell. They ran full-page advertisements in several US newspapers, but by noon, they issued a statement confirming it was a joke. This led to public outrage and protests. In response, to apologize, Taco Bell pledged $50,000 for the maintenance of the Liberty Bell.

TACO BELL BREAKFAST SALSA

Typically Served With: Breakfast Crunchwraps

Taco Bell introduced their breakfast menu in 2014 to compete with their fast-food rivals. They included breakfast tacos, burritos, and their signature breakfast item, the Breakfast Crunchwrap, to great success. In 2017, Taco Bell added to the menu their vividly yellow packets of mildly spiced and tomatoey Breakfast Salsa. The sauce was developed to be the perfect accompaniment to cheesy eggs, breakfast tacos, or toasted breakfast wraps. This salsa has some small chunks, making it different from Taco Bell's other sauce packets, and with this recipe it can be enjoyed anytime!

YIELDS 1 CUP, 2 TABLESPOONS PER SERVING

1/2 cup water
1/4 cup tomato paste
1/4 cup drained diced canned tomatoes, chopped into small pieces
2 teaspoons white vinegar
1 tablespoon finely chopped pickled jalapeño
2 teaspoons grated yellow onion
1/4 teaspoon garlic powder
1/4 teaspoon chili powder
1/4 teaspoon light soy sauce
1/8 teaspoon granulated sugar

1. Combine all ingredients in a 1-quart saucepan and stir well to combine. Heat mixture over medium-low heat and cook, stirring constantly, until mixture comes to a simmer, 6–8 minutes. Remove from heat and cool to room temperature.
2. Transfer mixture to a glass jar with a tight-fitting lid and refrigerate at least 4 hours before serving. Store up to 4 days in the refrigerator.

TACO BELL CREAMY JALAPEÑO SAUCE

Typically Served With: Chicken Quesadilla

Taco Bell's Creamy Jalapeño Sauce has devoted fans. Some so much so that they try (and sometimes succeed!) to buy this sauce by the bag from Taco Bell. Rather than heading down to your local Taco Bell, you can try this recipe instead. Sour cream and the brine from the jar of pickled jalapeños give this sauce a refreshing zip, while the spices and mayonnaise add richness and depth. If you want the sauce to have more zip, add a teaspoon or two of more jalapeño brine. If you want the sauce to be a bit thinner in texture without changing the flavor, whisk in a tablespoon of water.

YIELDS 1⅓ CUPS, 2 TABLESPOONS PER SERVING

½ cup sour cream
½ cup mayonnaise
¼ cup finely chopped pickled jalapeño
1 tablespoon jalapeño brine
2 teaspoons chili powder
1 teaspoon onion powder
½ teaspoon granulated sugar
½ teaspoon paprika
¼ teaspoon garlic powder
¼ teaspoon ground cumin
¼ teaspoon sea salt

Combine all ingredients in a medium bowl and whisk to combine. Transfer mixture to an airtight container and refrigerate at least 4 hours before serving. Store up to 5 days in the refrigerator.

Taco Bell

Glen Bell opened a burger stand—Bell's Hamburgers—in 1948 across from a Mexican restaurant that sold crispy tacos. Seeing their popularity, he decided to learn how to make the same kind of tacos and opened his new stand in 1954, called Taco-Tia. The first Taco Bell restaurant eventually opened in 1962.

TACO BELL CREAMY JALAPEÑO SAUCE

TACO BELL MEXICAN PIZZA SAUCE

Typically Served With: Mexican Pizza

When Taco Bell introduced their Mexican Pizza—originally called the Pizzazz Pizza—in 1985, it was a big hit! The layers of crisp tortillas and beef and the tangy tomato topping covered in cheese, lettuce, and tomato took all the best aspects of pizza and merged them with a taco. Much to the dismay of its many fans, the Mexican Pizza was discontinued in 2020 with Taco Bell citing the packaging as the primary reason. Mexican Pizza lovers were outraged, and one petition to bring it back got over 200,000 signatures! In 2022, the Mexican Pizza returned, much to the delight of its fans.

YIELDS ½ CUP, ¼ CUP PER SERVING

⅓ cup chunky red salsa
2 tablespoons crushed tomatoes
½ teaspoon chili powder
½ teaspoon dried oregano
¼ teaspoon onion powder
¼ teaspoon garlic powder

Combine all ingredients in a small bowl and mix well to combine. Use immediately or cover and refrigerate up to 3 days.

TACO BELL MILD SAUCE

Typically Served As: General Dipping Sauce

This sauce, offered in small blister packets decorated with clever sayings in Taco Bell restaurants, is perfect for those who want a bit of zip without strong spicy heat. Mild Sauce is a tangy tomato-based sauce flavored with chili powder, spices, and vinegar. The lineup of sauces Taco Bell has available for garnishing your menu favorites includes Hot, Fire, and Diablo, as well as a special Breakfast Salsa (a recipe you'll find in this chapter) served primarily with their breakfast menu. There have been other sauces in Taco Bell's history, including Verde Salsa and Fire Roasted.

YIELDS 1 CUP, 2 TABLESPOONS PER SERVING

1 cup water
3 tablespoons tomato paste
1½ teaspoons chili powder
1 teaspoon cornstarch
1 teaspoon white vinegar
½ teaspoon salt
⅛ teaspoon garlic powder
⅛ teaspoon onion powder
⅛ teaspoon cayenne pepper

1. Add all ingredients to a blender and purée 30 seconds. Transfer to a 2-quart saucepan.
2. Heat pan over medium-low heat, stirring constantly, until sauce simmers, about 5 minutes. Reduce heat to low and simmer 2 minutes or until sauce is glossy.
3. Remove from heat and cool to room temperature, then transfer to a glass jar with a tight-fitting lid. Use immediately or store up to 7 days in the refrigerator.

Taco Bell Sauce Packet Sayings

Prior to 2004, Taco Bell sauce packets only displayed the company logo and the name of the sauce on the front. To make them more fun for customers, the company decided to add clever sayings to each packet, giving sauce fans something extra to enjoy along with the tasty contents.

TACO BELL RED SAUCE

Typically Served With: Burrito Supreme

If you love Taco Bell's Bean Burrito, Burrito Supreme, or Pintos N Cheese, then you have had their signature red sauce. It is Taco Bell's take on traditional enchilada sauce made with tomato paste, chili powder, and spices cooked until the spices bloom and develop a rich flavor. The sauce is also popular ordered on the side as a dipping sauce for the Crunchwrap Supreme or drizzled over Nachos BellGrande or soft or crunchy tacos. If you prefer a mild sauce, be sure to use a mild chili powder.

YIELDS 1 CUP, 2 TABLESPOONS PER SERVING

1 tablespoon vegetable oil
1 tablespoon all-purpose flour
2 tablespoons tomato paste
1 tablespoon chili powder
1 cup water
1/2 teaspoon onion powder
1/2 teaspoon paprika
1/4 teaspoon ground cumin
1/4 teaspoon garlic powder
1/4 teaspoon sea salt
1/4 teaspoon cayenne pepper
1/4 teaspoon granulated sugar

1. In a 2-quart saucepan over medium heat, add oil. Once oil starts to shimmer, add flour and cook 1 minute or until flour is very lightly golden. Add tomato paste and chili powder and stir to combine. Cook, stirring constantly, 30 seconds.
2. Reduce heat to low, then whisk in water. Once water is fully whisked in, add remaining ingredients. Increase heat to medium and cook, stirring occasionally, until mixture comes just to a boil, about 5 minutes.
3. Remove pan from heat and cool 1 minute before serving. Store leftover sauce in a glass jar with a tight-fitting lid up to 7 days in the refrigerator.

TACO BELL SPICY RANCH

Typically Served As: General Dipping Sauce

Taco Bell has offered Spicy Ranch at various times throughout their history to pair with different menu items, such as their Crispy Chicken Nuggets. Taco Bell Spicy Ranch is creamy and cool but has a kick that will sneak up on you as you keep eating it. While great on tacos, chalupas, and quesadillas, it is also delicious on a crisp taco salad or with warm tortilla chips as a dip. You can enjoy this after 4 hours of chilling time, but if you can wait 24 hours, you will be rewarded with more robust flavors.

YIELDS 1 CUP, 2 TABLESPOONS PER SERVING

½ cup sour cream
¼ cup low-fat buttermilk
2 tablespoons mayonnaise
1 tablespoon hot pepper sauce, such as Tabasco
1 teaspoon freshly squeezed lime juice
½ teaspoon onion powder
¼ teaspoon dried dill
¼ teaspoon ground black pepper
¼ teaspoon garlic powder
¼ teaspoon sea salt
¼ teaspoon cayenne pepper
¼ teaspoon dried parsley

Add all ingredients to a food processor and pulse 5 or 6 times to combine. Transfer to a container with an airtight lid and refrigerate at least 4 hours before serving. Store up to 7 days in the refrigerator.

WENDY'S CREAMY SRIRACHA SAUCE

Typically Served With: Chicken Nuggets

Fans of Wendy's Creamy Sriracha Sauce were dismayed to learn the sauce was being discontinued in 2021 in favor of Ghost Pepper Ranch Sauce (Chapter 7). Some people were so upset with the change that they shared on social media they would no longer eat at Wendy's! If you're one of those loyal fans, this recipe might be just what you're looking for. The secret to this sauce is the lemon juice, which adds a bright flavor that cuts the richness of the mayonnaise and spice of the sriracha.

YIELDS 1⅛ CUPS, 2 TABLESPOONS PER SERVING

1 cup mayonnaise
2 tablespoons sriracha
1 teaspoon fresh-squeezed lemon juice
½ teaspoon honey
½ teaspoon onion powder
¼ teaspoon garlic powder
¼ teaspoon sea salt

In a small bowl, add all ingredients and whisk until well combined. Cover and refrigerate at least 4 hours before serving. Store up to 7 days in the refrigerator.

Sriracha Shortage

In 2017, due to a rupture in the partnership between popular sriracha manufacturer Huy Fong Foods and Underwood Ranches, the supplier of the red jalapeños used in sriracha, Huy Fong had to find a new supplier. They turned to a Mexican supplier, but that year the harvest was not up to their standards. Since then, sriracha has suffered intermittent shortages and can be difficult to find.

WHATABURGER SPICY KETCHUP

Typically Served With: French Fries

Whataburger is to Texans what In-N-Out Burger is to Californians. The chain is known for their limited-time menu drops, including burgers, fried pies, breakfast sandwiches, chicken sandwiches, and sauces. One of their most popular sauces is their proprietary ketchup, a recipe that yields a sweet and tangy ketchup that fans crave. In 2012, Whataburger released what arguably became their most popular limited-time menu item with a spicy version of their famous ketchup made with jalapeños for a bit of fiery kick. It was such a hit that a year later, the chain added it permanently to the menu!

YIELDS 1 CUP, 2 TABLESPOONS PER SERVING

2 cups water
1 large jalapeño, stem and seeds removed
1 (6-ounce) can tomato paste
2 tablespoons white vinegar
1 teaspoon granulated sugar
½ teaspoon onion powder
¼ teaspoon garlic powder
¼ teaspoon sea salt

1. In a 2-quart saucepan over medium-high heat, add water and jalapeño. Bring water to a boil, then reduce heat to medium-low, cover, and cook until jalapeño is very tender, about 20 minutes.
2. Once tender, remove jalapeño from water and add to a blender along with the remaining ingredients; discard water. Purée on high 30 seconds, scrape down sides of blender, then purée again 20 seconds.
3. Strain mixture through a fine mesh strainer in the same saucepan, gently pressing mixture through strainer with a spatula. Heat pan over medium-low heat and cook, stirring constantly, until ketchup thickens to your preference, 5–8 minutes.
4. Transfer ketchup to a glass jar with a tight-fitting lid and refrigerate 24 hours before serving. Store up to 7 days in the refrigerator.

Make It Easy

Want this ketchup in a flash? Simmer the jalapeño as directed in the recipe and purée it with 1 cup of your favorite brand of prepared ketchup along with ¼ teaspoon each of garlic powder and onion powder. This will keep for 7 days stored in a glass jar with a tight-fitting lid in the refrigerator.

CHAPTER 3

FROM TENDERS TO WINGS: CHICKEN DIPPING SAUCES

Chicken is big business, but delicious sauces for chicken may be even bigger business! Fried chicken paired with a tasty dipping sauce can't be beat, and the better the sauces, the more likely guests will return again and again. Fans are more than happy to share their favorite dipping sauces online. Raising Cane's Cane's Sauce is a prime example of the power a viral chicken tender dipping sauce can have. It has added to Raising Cane's popularity online, and that translates into more sales. This chapter features recipes for some of the most popular—and in some cases, the most viral—sauces and dips for chicken. You will find classic sweet and sour sauces like McDonald's Sweet 'N Sour Sauce and Chick-fil-A Polynesian Sauce, creamy sauces like Wingstop Ranch and Bojangles Bo Sauce, plus savory gravies like Jollibee Gravy and Dairy Queen Country Gravy, all perfect for dipping and drizzling over your favorite chicken dishes. So, next time you are planning on chicken, consider making a few of these delicious chicken dipping sauces!

BOJANGLES BO SAUCE

Typically Served With: Chicken Supremes

Founded in 1977 as Bojangles' Famous Chicken 'n Biscuits, today Bojangles is known for fried chicken (or chicken tenders depending on your location), buttery biscuits, sandwiches, breakfast sandwiches, and sides dishes known as "fixin's." They also have a variety of dipping sauces, with the most popular being their Bo Sauce. It is a creamy and tangy sauce with a bit of horseradish for heat. It was inexplicably discontinued in 2022, causing an uproar from fans who wanted their cult-favorite dip back. Good news for them: It was added back to the menu in 2024!

YIELDS 1 CUP, 2 TABLESPOONS PER SERVING

1 cup mayonnaise
1 tablespoon prepared horseradish
1 tablespoon finely minced red bell pepper
1 teaspoon paprika
1 teaspoon granulated sugar
1/2 teaspoon lemon juice
1/2 teaspoon apple cider vinegar
1/2 teaspoon onion powder
1/4 teaspoon garlic powder
1/4 teaspoon ground black pepper

Whisk all ingredients together in a medium bowl. Transfer to an airtight container and refrigerate 4 hours before serving. Store up to 7 days in the refrigerator.

Fresh Biscuits

Bojangles is famous for their delicious fried chicken and buttery biscuits. To ensure customers have the freshest biscuits possible, the chain bakes them fresh every 20 minutes. They do not use frozen or pre-made biscuits. Instead, they are mixed and cut fresh by Master Biscuit Makers!

BURGER KING ZESTY DIPPING SAUCE

Typically Served With: Chicken Nuggets

This signature dipping sauce at Burger King was introduced in 2001 as part of a new promotion for their onion rings, but it quickly became popular with guests for dipping anything and everything on the menu! Truly, it can be used for onion rings, chicken nuggets, chicken fries, and more. It is also delicious on burgers or for dipping French fries. This sauce is not spicy, but if you want to add a bit of heat, you can whisk in 1⁄4–1 teaspoon of your favorite hot pepper sauce or cayenne pepper.

YIELDS 1 CUP, 2 TABLESPOONS PER SERVING

3⁄4 cup mayonnaise
2 tablespoons ketchup
1 tablespoon Dijon mustard
1 tablespoon prepared horseradish
1 teaspoon granulated sugar
1 teaspoon lemon juice
1⁄2 teaspoon white vinegar
1⁄4 teaspoon soy sauce

Whisk all ingredients together in a medium bowl. Transfer to an airtight container and refrigerate 4 hours before serving. Store up to 7 days in the refrigerator.

CHICK-FIL-A HONEY MUSTARD SAUCE

Typically Served With: Chick-fil-A Nuggets

Added in 1984, Chick-fil-A Honey Mustard dipping sauce is a longtime favorite with its sweet and savory flavor. It was introduced so guests could flavor their chicken nuggets, also introduced in the 1980s. They knew what they were doing! Their Honey Mustard is perfect for dunking chicken nuggets—one of their most popular menu items (you can find a recipe for Chick-fil-A Nuggets in Chapter 10)—or chicken strips, or even for drizzling on their cult-favorite sandwiches. This sauce also makes a great dressing for chicken wraps or a glaze for baked or roasted chicken as it comes out of the oven.

YIELDS 1 CUP, 2 TABLESPOONS PER SERVING

1/2 cup mayonnaise
3 tablespoons Dijon mustard
3 tablespoons honey
1 tablespoon white vinegar
1 teaspoon water
1/4 teaspoon onion powder
1/4 teaspoon garlic powder
1/8 teaspoon turmeric

Whisk all ingredients together in a medium bowl. Transfer to an airtight container and refrigerate 4 hours before serving. Store up to 7 days in the refrigerator.

Vegan Alternatives

Most creamy sauces can be made vegan by swapping traditional mayonnaise or sour cream with a plant-based alternative. Honey can be swapped with agave or corn syrup, or you can use one of the vegan honey alternatives on the market. Vegan honey mustard is great on salads or for dunking plant-based chicken nuggets.

CHICK-FIL-A HONEY ROASTED BBQ SAUCE

Typically Served With: Chick-fil-A Nuggets

Chick-fil-A Honey Roasted BBQ Sauce is creamy and sweet with a smoky flavor and arguably—if people on Internet forums are to be believed—the best sauce Chick-fil-A offers! The secret to this sauce is a little bit of pineapple juice that gives it a bit of fruity sharpness. It also gives the sauce a slightly refreshing flavor. You can use any barbecue sauce you like here, but one that has a bold, smoky flavor works best. This sauce is perfect for grilled chicken sandwiches or as a dip for grilled or fried chicken. It is also great as a potato salad dressing.

YIELDS 1 CUP, 2 TABLESPOONS PER SERVING

1/2 cup mayonnaise
1/3 cup barbecue sauce
3 tablespoons honey
2 tablespoons yellow mustard
1 tablespoon pineapple juice
1/4 teaspoon smoked paprika
1/4 teaspoon onion powder
1/8 teaspoon garlic powder

Whisk all ingredients together in a medium bowl. Transfer to an airtight container and refrigerate 4 hours before serving. Store up to 7 days in the refrigerator.

CHICK-FIL-A POLYNESIAN SAUCE

Typically Served With: Chick-fil-A Nuggets

Chick-fil-A Polynesian Sauce is a sweet and tangy dipping sauce Chick-fil-A introduced in 1984 to accompany their chicken nuggets. Today it remains one of the most popular dipping sauces they offer. One ingredient that sets this sauce apart from other sweet and sour dipping sauces is the addition of tomato, which adds to the tangy flavor. In this recipe the tomato comes in the form of ketchup, which also includes the sugar and vinegar that are part of the famous sauce too. If you prefer, you can swap honey or agave syrup for corn syrup, but do not use maple syrup as it has too strong a flavor.

YIELDS 1 CUP, 2 TABLESPOONS PER SERVING

1/3 cup ketchup
1/4 cup corn syrup
1/4 cup vegetable oil
2 tablespoons apple cider vinegar
1/2 teaspoon paprika
1/4 teaspoon garlic powder
1/4 teaspoon onion powder
1/4 teaspoon dry mustard powder

Whisk all ingredients together in a medium bowl. Transfer to an airtight container and refrigerate 4 hours before serving. Store up to 7 days in the refrigerator.

Sweet and Sour Story

Asian cuisine has a long history of balancing sweet and sour flavors. When Chinese immigrants came to the United States in the nineteenth century, they brought these recipes with them and adapted them to suit Western palates and ingredients. Now, sweet and sour sauces are incredibly popular, even if they are different from their origins.

CHICK-FIL-A SAUCE

Typically Served With: Chick-fil-A Nuggets

The story behind this fan favorite dipping sauce starts in the 1980s, when Virginia Chick-fil-A franchise owner Hugh Fleming wanted to make a sauce for his customers to dip their nuggets in that was not just ketchup. As the story goes, Hugh initially served honey mustard mixed with coleslaw dressing, but when an employee added some barbecue sauce to the mix, the sauce that he called Fleming's Own: The Original Fredericksburg Nugget Sauce was born. This sauce recipe was his secret until 2007, when he gave it to Chick-fil-A corporate for free, and it was rolled out nationally in 2008.

YIELDS 1 CUP, 2 TABLESPOONS PER SERVING

1/2 cup mayonnaise
1/4 cup hickory-smoked barbecue sauce
2 tablespoons honey
2 tablespoons Dijon mustard
2 teaspoons lemon juice
1 teaspoon apple cider vinegar
1/4 teaspoon paprika
1/4 teaspoon garlic powder
1/4 teaspoon sea salt

Whisk all ingredients together in a medium bowl. Transfer to an airtight container and refrigerate 4 hours before serving. Store up to 7 days in the refrigerator.

CHICK-FIL-A SAUCE

DAIRY QUEEN COUNTRY GRAVY

Typically Served With: Chicken Strip Basket

Dairy Queen introduced their Country Gravy as an accompaniment to their newly introduced Chicken Strip Basket in 1995. At Texas DQ locations, the gravy is served with the Chick'n Strip and Steak Finger Country Baskets and dubbed "the best cream gravy anywhere." For the full restaurant experience at home, serve this with chicken tenders, French fries, and buttered Texas toast. If the gravy is too thick, you can stir in 2–3 tablespoons of additional milk to loosen it. If you want the gravy to be richer in flavor, substitute 1/2 cup of the whole milk for heavy cream.

YIELDS 2 CUPS, 1/2 CUP PER SERVING

1/4 cup unsalted butter
1/4 cup all-purpose flour
2 cups whole milk
1 teaspoon ground black pepper
1/2 teaspoon sea salt

1. In a 10-inch nonstick skillet over medium heat, add butter. Once butter is melted and foaming, add flour and whisk with a silicone whisk to combine. Cook, whisking constantly, 2 minutes or until flour starts to turn lightly golden brown. Reduce heat to low and slowly whisk in milk until smooth. Whisk in pepper and salt.
2. Once gravy is smooth, increase heat to medium and cook until gravy comes to a boil and thickens to your preference, 3–5 minutes. Gravy will thicken as it cools. Serve immediately.
3. Transfer leftover gravy to an airtight container and store up to 3 days in the refrigerator. Reheat gravy in a 10-inch nonstick skillet over medium-low heat until hot and bubbling, about 5 minutes, before serving.

Liquid Gold

If you have made fried chicken or chicken fried steak, you should have some fry oil left over. If you do, you have liquid gold on your hands! You can swap your frying oil for the butter in this recipe. It will give your gravy a richer, more savory flavor.

IHOP SAUCE

Typically Served With: Buttermilk Crispy Chicken Strips & Fries

IHOP may be best known for pancakes, flavorful syrups, and other breakfast items, but they have a large lunch and dinner menu that is also very popular. On that menu is their crave-worthy IHOP Sauce. You can order it with menu items like the Appetizer Sampler, Chicken & Waffles, or Buttermilk Crispy Chicken Strips & Fries. The sauce is actually very simple to make—just equal parts mayonnaise, ketchup, and yellow mustard—but the flavor is complex. For fans of the sauce, this recipe makes it easy to have it anytime at home.

YIELDS 1¼ CUPS, 2 TABLESPOONS PER SERVING

½ cup mayonnaise
½ cup ketchup
½ cup yellow mustard

Whisk all ingredients together in a medium bowl. Transfer to an airtight container and refrigerate 4 hours before serving. Store up to 7 days in the refrigerator.

International House of Pancakes

Originating in Toluca Lake, California, in 1958 as the International House of Pancakes—shortened to IHOP in 1973—the chain became popular for tasty breakfasts. What makes it "International"? The inclusion of menu items such as crepes, Belgian waffles, and French toast.

JACK IN THE BOX GOOD GOOD SAUCE

Typically Served As: General Dipping Sauce

Jack in the Box has a wide variety of sauces available to order, but one of the tastiest is their Good Good Sauce. It has a creamy and tangy flavor with a bit of an herbal taste that makes it irresistible. To re-create it at home, you will need a little dry buttermilk ranch seasoning mix. You can buy packets of the mix at the grocery store in the salad dressing and condiments aisle, or find it at warehouse stores in larger-format containers with the spices. This recipe can be made into Spicy Good Good Sauce by adding 2 teaspoons of your favorite hot pepper sauce.

YIELDS 1 CUP, 2 TABLESPOONS PER SERVING

3/4 cup mayonnaise
1 tablespoon plus 1 teaspoon yellow mustard
1 tablespoon ketchup
1 tablespoon spicy barbecue sauce
1 teaspoon white vinegar
1/2 teaspoon dry buttermilk ranch seasoning mix, such as Hidden Valley
1/4 teaspoon onion powder
1/4 teaspoon ground black pepper
1/4 teaspoon celery seed

Whisk all ingredients together in a medium bowl. Transfer to an airtight container and refrigerate 4 hours before serving. Store up to 7 days in the refrigerator.

JOLLIBEE GRAVY

Typically Served With: Chickenjoy

Jollibee is the most popular fast-food brand in the Philippines. They have more than 1,700 locations globally as of 2025. In 1998 their first US location opened in Daly City, California, and today the chain has over seventy-five US locations. Jollibee is most popular for its fried chicken, called Chickenjoy, which is served with various sides, including a savory brown gravy that people love. The gravy can be ordered as an à la carte side and used for dunking fried chicken or fries or for drizzling over mashed potatoes. The secret to the savory flavor of this gravy is a little bit of soy sauce, so don't leave it out!

YIELDS 4 CUPS, 1/2 CUP PER SERVING

1/4 cup unsalted butter
1/4 cup all-purpose flour
3 cups chicken stock
1 cup whole milk
1 teaspoon soy sauce
1 teaspoon white pepper
1/2 teaspoon sea salt

1. In a 2-quart pot over medium heat, add butter. Once butter is melted and foaming, add flour and whisk with a silicone whisk to combine. Cook, whisking constantly, 3 minutes or until flour turns lightly golden brown. Reduce heat to low and slowly whisk in chicken stock until smooth. Whisk in milk, soy sauce, pepper, and salt.
2. Once gravy is smooth, increase heat to medium and cook until gravy comes to a boil and thickens to your preference, 5–8 minutes. Gravy will thicken as it cools. Serve immediately.
3. Transfer leftover gravy to an airtight container and store up to 3 days in the refrigerator. Reheat gravy in the microwave in 30-second intervals, stirring well between each interval, until steaming hot before serving.

International Menus

When Jollibee enters a new market, they bring their classic menu items like Chickenjoy, Yumburgers, Palabok Fiesta, and Jolly Spaghetti, and then tailor the rest of the menu for local tastes. The US menu includes chicken tenders and is overall smaller, but some individual items—like the Yumburgers—are bigger.

KFC BUFFALO RANCH

Typically Served As: General Dipping Sauce

In 2022, KFC introduced its Buffalo Ranch sauce. It was billed as the perfect blend of cool creamy ranch and spicy buffalo sauce. The rollout included a partnership with the dating app Tinder, which noted users often bond over favorite foods and restaurants. They had a "What's Your Sauce Style?" quiz KFC fans could take to help them match with the sauce of their dreams. This promotion also included a chance to win a Saucy Dream Date with tickets for a Jack Harlow concert and an all-expense-paid trip for two. Pretty saucy!

YIELDS 1 CUP, 2 TABLESPOONS PER SERVING

½ cup mayonnaise
¼ cup low-fat buttermilk
¼ cup buffalo wing sauce, such as Frank's RedHot
½ teaspoon onion powder
¼ teaspoon dried dill
¼ teaspoon ground black pepper
¼ teaspoon garlic powder
¼ teaspoon sea salt

Whisk all ingredients together in a medium bowl. Transfer to an airtight container and refrigerate 4 hours before serving. Store up to 5 days in the refrigerator.

Kentucky for Christmas

In 1974, KFC Japan ran a "Kentucky for Christmas" marketing campaign that falsely claimed Americans ate fried chicken at Christmas. It is rumored the idea came when a tourist claimed that since they could not get turkey in Japan, the next best thing was KFC. Today, customers order meals weeks in advance to be sure they get their Christmas KFC!

KFC COMEBACK SAUCE

Typically Served As: General Dipping Sauce

Having the most viral and craveable fried chicken has become big business! KFC has always been one of the major players in the fried chicken game, and in 2024 they added another weapon in their arsenal: Comeback Sauce. Introduced as a dip for their Original Recipe Chicken Tenders and Secret Recipe Fries, the sauce has a bold flavor designed to complement their famous eleven herbs and spices. Taking a jab at their competitors, they cheekily noted that their chicken with Comeback Sauce is available seven days a week, and you could choose chicken featuring their secret recipe rather than Louisiana spices.

YIELDS 1 CUP, 2 TABLESPOONS PER SERVING

2/3 cup mayonnaise
3 tablespoons ketchup
1 tablespoon hot pepper sauce
1/2 teaspoon Worcestershire sauce
1/2 teaspoon ground black pepper
1/4 teaspoon garlic powder
1/4 teaspoon molasses
1/8 teaspoon onion powder
1/8 teaspoon dried oregano

Whisk all ingredients together in a medium bowl. Transfer to an airtight container and refrigerate 4 hours before serving. Store up to 7 days in the refrigerator.

Top Secret Recipe

KFC is best known for their Original Recipe fried chicken made with their top secret blend of eleven herbs and spices. The recipe, known to only two executives at any one time, is one of the most guarded trade secrets in the restaurant industry, locked in a secure vault with motion sensors and cameras recording 24/7.

KFC GRAVY

Typically Served With: Mashed Potatoes

Kathleen "Kay" Kerr of Alberta, Canada, is a person you may not know, but if you love KFC's famous gravy, you will want to remember her! Kay and her husband, Jack, owned four KFC franchise locations in Alberta, and Kay had been working on a way to reduce the cook time of the chain's gravy. She eventually found a way to reduce the cooking time from 30 minutes to just 2. Her gravy innovation was so impressive, she was invited to stay with Colonel Sanders at his home, where she shared the recipe for his approval. He did approve, and the recipe is still the one they use to this day!

YIELDS 1 CUP, 2 TABLESPOONS PER SERVING

3 tablespoons vegetable oil
3 tablespoons all-purpose flour
1 (10-ounce) can condensed chicken stock
1½ cups chicken broth
⅛ teaspoon Accent Flavor Enhancer
⅛ teaspoon ground black pepper
1 chicken bouillon cube
¼ teaspoon ground sage

1. Heat a 1-quart saucepan over medium-low heat. Add oil and, once shimmering, whisk in flour. Cook, stirring constantly, 5 minutes or until mixture is a nutty brown.
2. Remove from heat and slowly whisk in stock, broth, Accent Flavor Enhancer, pepper, bouillon cube, and sage until smooth.
3. Return to stove and bring to a boil over medium heat. Reduce heat to low and allow gravy to thicken to desired consistency, 3–5 minutes. Serve immediately.
4. Transfer leftover gravy to an airtight container and store in refrigerator up to 3 days. Reheat gravy in the microwave in 30-second intervals, stirring well between each interval, until steaming hot.

KFC GRAVY

KFC SAUCE

Typically Served As: General Dipping Sauce

KFC Sauce was introduced in 2020 as a replacement for their Finger Lickin' Good Sauce—a change made as KFC discontinued their slogan "It's Finger Lickin' Good" during a time when the slogan did not fit with the environment of heightened hygiene awareness. Sweet and tangy with a hint of smoke, this sauce was created to complement their chicken tenders but is also good drizzled over their Original Recipe or Extra Crispy fried chicken. Deli mustard, also known as spicy brown mustard, has a somewhat coarse texture, but you can swap it for Dijon.

YIELDS 3/4 CUP, 2 TABLESPOONS PER SERVING

1/2 cup mayonnaise
2 tablespoons packed light brown sugar
1 tablespoon deli mustard
1 teaspoon molasses
1 teaspoon white vinegar
1/4 teaspoon smoked paprika
1/4 teaspoon onion powder
1/4 teaspoon garlic powder
1/4 teaspoon Worcestershire sauce
1/8 teaspoon ground black pepper

Whisk all ingredients together in a medium bowl. Transfer to an airtight container and refrigerate 4 hours before serving. Store up to 7 days in the refrigerator.

MCDONALD'S SWEET 'N SOUR SAUCE

Typically Served With: Chicken McNuggets

Perhaps the most iconic dipping sauce on the McDonald's menu, and ubiquitous with chicken nuggets, Sweet 'N Sour Sauce hit the menu in 1983 along with three other sauces for their McNuggets. McDonald's Sweet 'N Sour Sauce is based loosely on American-style Chinese sweet and sour sauce served with fried chicken or pork. The McDonald's version uses a surprising ingredient—apricot purée! The apricot gives the sauce a mild, fruity flavor that is less tangy than the sauce served in American Chinese restaurants.

YIELDS 1 CUP, 2 TABLESPOONS PER SERVING

3/4 cup apricot preserves
2 tablespoons rice vinegar
2 tablespoons light corn syrup
1 tablespoon water
2 teaspoons corn starch
2 teaspoons light soy sauce
1 teaspoon yellow mustard
1/4 teaspoon garlic power
1/4 teaspoon paprika

1. Add all ingredients to a blender and purée 30 seconds.
2. Transfer mixture to a 1-quart saucepan and heat over medium heat, stirring constantly, until mixture comes to a boil, 3–5 minutes. Remove from heat and cool completely to room temperature.
3. Transfer to an airtight container and refrigerate 4 hours before serving. Store up to 7 days in the refrigerator.

Perfectly Peachy

If you like, you can swap half or all the apricot in this recipe with peach preserves. The recipe used by McDonald's lists apricot and/or peach in the ingredients, so feel free to play around with this swap until you find a ratio you like best!

POPEYES BLACKENED RANCH SAUCE

Typically Served With: Classic Boneless Wings

Joining the Popeyes menu in 2012, Blackened Ranch Sauce became a favorite of people who enjoy creamy ranch dressing with a spicy kick. The sauce is a big fan favorite and often tops the rankings of Popeyes sauces. The sauce starts with a ranch base and adds Cajun blackening seasoning and herbs. It is great as a dip but can also be used as a salad dressing. This sauce has a kick from the cayenne pepper, but if you don't like it spicy, you can leave it out or swap it for sweet paprika.

YIELDS 1 CUP, 2 TABLESPOONS PER SERVING

3/4 cup mayonnaise
3 tablespoons sour cream
3 tablespoons buttermilk
1/2 teaspoon onion powder
1/2 teaspoon ground black pepper
1/4 teaspoon dried dill
1/4 teaspoon garlic powder
1/4 teaspoon Cajun seasoning
1/4 teaspoon smoked paprika
1/4 teaspoon cayenne pepper
1/4 teaspoon dried oregano

Whisk all ingredients together in a medium bowl. Transfer to an airtight container and refrigerate 4 hours before serving. Store up to 7 days in the refrigerator.

POPEYES BLACKENED RANCH SAUCE

POPEYES MARDI GRAS MUSTARD

Typically Served With: Classic Tenders

Popeyes has a strong lineup of sauces, and one of the more popular is their Mardi Gras Mustard. Named after the ultimate party, this sauce is a creamy blend of creole mustard, mayonnaise, and spices, with a hint of sweetness. While the sauce is delicious on chicken tenders and nuggets, its zesty flavor is also great with other fried foods like French fries and onion rings. It would also pair perfectly with fresh soft pretzels! If you can't find creole mustard, you can swap it for deli or spicy mustard.

YIELDS 1 CUP, 2 TABLESPOONS PER SERVING

½ cup mayonnaise
¼ cup creole mustard
2 tablespoons Dijon mustard
1 tablespoon prepared horseradish
1 teaspoon packed light brown sugar
¼ teaspoon Cajun seasoning
⅛ teaspoon onion powder
⅛ teaspoon garlic powder

Whisk all ingredients together in a medium bowl. Transfer to an airtight container and refrigerate 4 hours before serving. Store up to 7 days in the refrigerator.

A Tale of Two Companies

Popeyes was founded in 1975 as Chicken on the Run in a suburb of New Orleans, Louisiana. Founder Alvin Copeland renamed the restaurant later that same year to Popeyes. Alvin also established Diversified Foods and Seasonings, which owned the recipes for the chain's seasonings. Popeyes acquired the recipes in 2014 for a reported $43 million!

POPEYES SWEET HEAT SAUCE

Typically Served With: Classic Tenders

Like their Mardi Gras Mustard or Blackened Ranch Sauce, their Sweet Heat Sauce was added to Popeyes' menu in 2012, which was an epic year for Popeyes sauces! This sauce is similar to a traditional buffalo sauce but with more sweetness. While it's a great dip, you can also use it as a marinade. For chicken, add the chicken to the mixture and chill for 30 minutes to 2 hours before cooking. For seafood like shrimp, marinate for 10 minutes before cooking. You can also use this as a glaze; just brush it over meat and seafood while grilling.

YIELDS 1¼ CUPS, 2 TABLESPOONS PER SERVING

½ cup hot pepper sauce, such as Tabasco
¼ cup packed light brown sugar
¼ cup honey
2 tablespoons white sugar
2 tablespoons corn syrup
1 teaspoon cayenne pepper
½ teaspoon Worcestershire sauce

1. Combine all ingredients in a 1-quart saucepan over medium heat. Cook, whisking constantly, until mixture starts to simmer, about 5 minutes. Remove from heat and cool to room temperature before serving.
2. Transfer leftover sauce to an airtight container and refrigerate. Store up to 7 days in the refrigerator. Let sauce come to room temperature before serving.

RAISING CANE'S CANE'S SAUCE

Typically Served With: Chicken Fingers

When you think of viral fast food you may think of Popeyes Classic Chicken Sandwich, McDonald's Szechuan Sauce, and—most recently—Raising Cane's Cane's Sauce. From TikTok and Instagram reels of people dunking whole tenders and buttery slices of Texas toast into large drink cups of the sauce, Cane's Sauce has become a staple of the mukbang community. The official recipe for the sauce is a closely held company secret despite people claiming to have it. This version is as close as it gets to hitting the drive-through for a large cup of sauce!

YIELDS 1 CUP, 2 TABLESPOONS PER SERVING

2/3 cup mayonnaise
1/4 cup ketchup
2 tablespoons Worcestershire sauce
2 teaspoons hot pepper sauce, such as Tabasco
1/4 teaspoon ground black pepper
1/4 teaspoon onion powder
1/4 teaspoon garlic powder
1/8 teaspoon creole seasoning

Whisk all ingredients together in a medium bowl. Transfer to an airtight container and refrigerate 24 hours before serving. Store up to 7 days in the refrigerator.

The Namesake

Did you know that Raising Cane's is named for founder Todd Graves' yellow Labrador Cane? When Todd was planning his chicken fingers restaurant in 1996 he brought his dog to the building site, and his friend suggested he name the restaurant Cane. The name has carried on today, and Cane III was born in 2017.

RAISING CANE'S CANE'S SAUCE

WHATABURGER BUTTERMILK RANCH

Typically Served With: Buffalo Ranch Chicken Strip Sandwich

Whataburger has developed a cult following for its limited-time sandwich and burger offerings. There is a rotating menu, and fans wait with enthusiasm for the announcement of the next sandwiches and burgers. Among the most popular is the Buffalo Ranch Chicken Strip Sandwich, which features crispy chicken tenders, Monterey jack cheese, buffalo sauce, and this creamy Buttermilk Ranch. It has a bit more herbs and spices than a typical ranch, so the flavor stands up to combining with tangy buffalo sauce and is very popular with fans. It is so popular that Whataburger sells it in bottles in select grocery stores!

YIELDS 1¼ CUPS, 3 TABLESPOONS PER SERVING

¾ cup mayonnaise
¼ tablespoons sour cream
¼ cup buttermilk
1 teaspoon lemon juice
1 teaspoon onion powder
½ teaspoon ground black pepper
½ teaspoon dried parsley
½ teaspoon dried chives
½ teaspoon dried dill
¼ teaspoon garlic powder
¼ teaspoon ground black pepper

Whisk all ingredients together in a medium bowl. Transfer to an airtight container and refrigerate 4 hours before serving. Store up to 7 days in the refrigerator.

What's in a Name?

Founded in Corpus Christi, Texas, in 1950, Whataburger started as a hamburger restaurant that has since expanded to over one thousand locations. The owner claimed he wanted to make a burger that was so tasty, customers would say, "What a burger!" And thus the name was chosen.

WINGSTOP RANCH

Typically Served With: Classic Bone-In Wings

Fans of Wingstop Ranch were delighted, and in some cases shocked, when they discovered a TikTok of a Wingstop worker making a batch of their famous Ranch. The worker was shown mixing giant containers of mayonnaise, cartons of buttermilk, and packets of ranch seasoning in a large tub. The comments varied from delight to how simple the recipe was to shock that it contained mayonnaise. Some eagle-eyed users identified the seasoning used—Hidden Valley Original Ranch! Tinkering with the ratios revealed the secret to the recipe for this book: adding more ranch seasoning than the Hidden Valley packet recipe typically calls for.

YIELDS 2 CUPS, 1/4 CUP PER SERVING

1 cup buttermilk
1 cup mayonnaise
1½ (1-ounce) packets Hidden Valley Original Ranch Seasoning, Salad Dressing & Recipe Mix

Whisk all ingredients together in a medium bowl. Transfer to an airtight container and refrigerate 4 hours before serving. Store up to 7 days in the refrigerator.

ZAXBYS ZAX SAUCE

Typically Served With: Chicken Fingerz

Famous for chicken tenders, wings, sandwiches, and a range of twelve different dipping sauces, Zaxbys is a Georgia-based fast-casual chain with over nine hundred locations across the Southern and Southwestern United States. Among the most popular sauces they offer is their peppery Zax Sauce. This sauce, one of the original sauces they offered when they opened in 1990, is peppery and zingy with a mild heat from a touch of hot pepper sauce. It is sold in small tubs in the restaurants, but with this recipe, you can make as much as you want!

YIELDS 1 CUP, 2 TABLESPOONS PER SERVING

2/3 cup mayonnaise
1/3 cup ketchup
2 teaspoons hot pepper sauce, such as Tabasco
2 teaspoons ground black pepper
1/2 teaspoon celery seed
1/2 teaspoon Worcestershire sauce
1/2 teaspoon onion powder
1/4 teaspoon granulated sugar
1/4 teaspoon garlic powder
1/4 teaspoon paprika
1/4 teaspoon white pepper

Whisk all ingredients together in a medium bowl. Transfer to an airtight container and refrigerate 4 hours before serving. Store up to 7 days in the refrigerator.

CHAPTER 4

BETWEEN TWO BUNS: BURGER AND SANDWICH SAUCES

Sandwich spreads, schmears, and burger sauces can make a good thing great! You are probably familiar with some of the most popular burger sauces and have most likely tried and loved a few. What makes a burger sauce popular is how it enhances the savory flavors of grilled beef and melty cheese while not overpowering any of the flavors that make a burger delicious. Burger sauces entered popular American culture thanks to McDonald's Big Mac and its highly popular sauce, and burger chains jumped on the trend! Along with burger sauces, there are sandwich spreads meant to pair with savory meats and cheeses, as on roast beef or loaded sub sandwiches. There are also flavored spreads and schmears to dress up bagels and other toasted breads. This chapter has all three—burger sauces, sandwich spreads, and schmears—with recipes for some of the classics. McDonald's Big Mac Sauce, Arby's Horsey Sauce, Sonic Chili, and the Reduced Fat Honey Almond Shmear from Einstein Bros. Bagels are just a few of the best known and best loved of these that you can now make at home!

ARBY'S BBQ DIPPING SAUCE

Typically Served With: Chicken Tenders

If your restaurant is famous for its meats, it just makes sense to have barbecue sauce too! Arby's offers two barbecue sauces, with their BBQ Dipping Sauce being the most popular choice for adding to all kinds of sandwiches. This was designed as a sandwich spread and dip for chicken tenders and fries. It has a sweet and tangy flavor with a hint of smokiness. The smoky flavor in this recipe comes from a touch of liquid smoke, but if you do not have any or prefer not to use it, you can swap in ½ teaspoon smoked paprika.

YIELDS 1 CUP, 2 TABLESPOONS PER SERVING

½ cup water
½ cup ketchup
2 tablespoons packed dark brown sugar
1 tablespoon tomato paste
1 tablespoon Worcestershire sauce
1 tablespoon apple cider vinegar
1 teaspoon onion powder
½ teaspoon garlic powder
½ teaspoon dry mustard powder
⅛ teaspoon liquid smoke

1. In a 2-quart saucepan over medium heat, combine all ingredients until well mixed. Bring mixture to a boil, then reduce heat to medium-low and simmer until sauce thickens to coat the back of a spoon, about 5 minutes. Remove from heat and cool 10 minutes before use.
2. Transfer leftovers to an airtight container and refrigerate. Store up to 7 days in the refrigerator. Reheat sauce in the microwave 30–50 seconds before use.

ARBY'S CHEDDAR CHEESE SAUCE

Typically Served With: Beef 'n Cheddar

In 1978, Arby's added the now massively popular Beef 'n Cheddar to their menu. This sandwich was a change from the original lineup that included only Swiss cheese as the cheese option. It was developed over several months by a group of franchisees who wanted to create the perfect roast beef and cheese sandwich. The sandwich was so popular that it is often the one most associated with the chain. Aside from topping roast beef sandwiches, this cheese sauce is good poured over French fries, used for dunking chips, or added to hamburgers or chicken or fish sandwiches.

YIELDS 3 CUPS, 1/3 CUP PER SERVING

2 tablespoons unsalted butter
2 tablespoons all-purpose flour
1 cup whole milk
3/4 cup shredded deli American cheese
1/2 cup shredded extra sharp Cheddar cheese
1/4 teaspoon sea salt
1/4 teaspoon white pepper

1. In a 2-quart saucepan over medium-heat, add butter. Once butter is melted and foaming, add flour and whisk to combine. Cook, whisking constantly, 2 minutes. Reduce heat to low and slowly whisk in milk until all milk is added and mixture is smooth.
2. Increase heat to medium and cook, whisking constantly, until mixture comes to a boil and thickens, about 8 minutes.
3. Reduce heat to low and add shredded cheeses in three increments, whisking well to make sure all cheese is melted before adding more. Once all cheese is added, whisk in salt and pepper. If sauce is too thick, whisk in more milk a tablespoon at a time until desired consistency is achieved. Serve immediately.

Arby's Has the Meats

"We Have the Meats" has been the Arby's slogan for over 10 years, with actor Ving Rhames providing the voice for the chain in commercials. Aside from roast beef, Arby's also sells turkey, brisket, and—in a stroke of irony—hamburgers since 2022.

ARBY'S HORSEY SAUCE

Typically Served With: Classic Roast Beef

Nothing pairs better with roast beef than horseradish, which is why Arby's includes this sauce on their menu. The sauce is a perfect blend of creamy and spicy from a kick of horseradish and a touch of dry mustard powder. A bit of sugar is added to balance the heat and prevent the sauce from being too overpowering. In 2024, Arby's launched a special promotion for their Horsey Sauce, introducing a limited-edition version with a chardonnay-flavored finish called Chardonneigh's Arby's Horsey Sauce. This unique sauce sold out quickly, and bottles were later listed resold by third-party resellers!

YIELDS 1¼ CUPS, 2 TABLESPOONS PER SERVING

1 cup mayonnaise
3 tablespoons prepared horseradish
1 tablespoon white vinegar
1 tablespoon water
1 tablespoon granulated sugar
¼ teaspoon dry mustard

1. Combine all ingredients in a blender and purée 30 seconds, occasionally scraping down the sides, until smooth and creamy.
2. Transfer to an airtight container and refrigerate 4 hours before serving. Store up to 5 days in the refrigerator.

ARBY'S RED RANCH

Typically Served With: Beef 'n Cheddar

If you have ever had an Arby's Roast Beef or Beef 'n Cheddar and noticed a sweet and tangy sauce, that is what Arby's calls Red Ranch. While they call it "ranch," it is not a creamy or an herb-flavored sauce. The flavor is more akin to French dressing. The sauce is ketchup based, with extra sugar and vinegar added, along with some spices for depth of flavor. Once blended, the sauce is simmered to reduce and let the flavors blend. This is delicious on roast beef sandwiches or hamburgers or used as a dipping sauce for chicken tenders, fries, or onion rings.

YIELDS 1½ CUPS, 2 TABLESPOONS PER SERVING

1 cup ketchup
⅓ cup apple cider vinegar
⅓ cup granulated sugar
½ teaspoon garlic powder
½ teaspoon onion powder
¼ teaspoon ground black pepper

1. Combine all ingredients in a blender and purée 30 seconds, occasionally scraping down the sides, until well combined.
2. Pour mixture in a 2-quart saucepan over medium-low heat. Cook, stirring often, until mixture comes to a low simmer. Cook, stirring constantly, until sauce reduces by ¼, about 15 minutes. Remove from heat and cool to room temperature before serving.
3. Transfer leftover sauce to an airtight container and refrigerate. Store up to 7 days in the refrigerator. Let sauce come to room temperature before serving.

Arby's Sauce Fandom

Arby's offers a wide array of sauces, and they change the lineup on a fairly regular basis. The sauces are so popular with fans that they will try them all and share their sauce rankings—often updated by year—online. People also like to share their favorite custom sauce combinations, like mixing Arby's and Horsey Sauces.

ARBY'S SAUCE

Typically Served With: Classic Roast Beef

Tart with a flavor that is a mix of sweet ketchup and ingredients reminiscent of vinegary barbecue sauce, Arby's Sauce is an iconic condiment so good, it was named after the restaurant chain when it was introduced in the 1970s. The flavor is mouthwatering and unique, and it complements savory meats like roast beef, beef brisket, and even fried and roasted chicken. The sauce is popular with fans, and you can find several Instagram and TikTok reels featuring the sauce in mukbangs, sauce rankings—or in one TikTok—the opening of a 50-pound box of sauce!

YIELDS 1½ CUPS, 2 TABLESPOONS PER SERVING

1 cup plus 2 tablespoons water, divided
½ cup ketchup
¼ cup apple cider vinegar
2 tablespoons Worcestershire sauce
2 tablespoons packed dark brown sugar
1 teaspoon garlic powder
½ teaspoon onion powder
½ teaspoon paprika
½ teaspoon hot pepper sauce, such as Tabasco
1 tablespoon cornstarch

1. In a blender, combine 1 cup water, ketchup, vinegar, Worcestershire sauce, brown sugar, garlic powder, onion powder, paprika, and hot pepper sauce. Purée 30 seconds.
2. Pour mixture in a 2-quart saucepan set over medium-low heat. Cook, stirring often, until mixture comes to a low simmer. Cook, stirring constantly, until sauce reduces by ¼, about 15 minutes.
3. In a small bowl, combine remaining water and cornstarch and then whisk into simmering sauce. Increase heat to medium and bring just to a boil to thicken, about 1 minute. Remove from heat and cool completely to room temperature before serving.
4. Transfer leftover sauce to an airtight container and refrigerate. Store up to 7 days in the refrigerator. Let sauce come to room temperature before serving.

ARBY'S SAUCE

CARL'S JR. CLASSIC SAUCE

Typically Served With: California Classic Double Cheeseburger

Carl's Jr. is famous for their restaurant-style burgers at reasonable prices, their viral commercials featuring popular influencers enjoying burgers while washing cars in slow motion, and their ability to take a trend and make it their own. This sauce, formerly known as Big Twin Sauce, is featured on some of their most popular burgers like their California Classic Double Cheeseburger and Big Angus Big Carl. It is a well-seasoned take on Thousand Island dressing, with plenty of sweet pickle relish and minced onion for texture and flavor. If you can make this sauce a day ahead, it will taste even better!

YIELDS 1 CUP, 2 TABLESPOONS PER SERVING

½ cup mayonnaise
2 tablespoons chili sauce
2 tablespoons ketchup
3 tablespoons sweet pickle relish
2 tablespoon minced yellow onion
½ teaspoon paprika
½ teaspoon lemon juice

In a medium bowl, combine all ingredients and fold to combine. Transfer to an airtight container and refrigerate 4 hours before serving. Store up to 5 days in the refrigerator.

Humble Beginnings

Carl's Jr. was founded with only $15 in savings and a loan of $311 on Carl Karcher's Plymouth. Yes, Carl, the namesake! Carl and his wife, Margaret, opened a hot dog cart in 1941 in Los Angeles, eventually adding burgers, and the cart grew into the restaurant chain that has over one thousand locations today.

EINSTEIN BROS. BAGELS ONION & CHIVE SHMEAR

Typically Served With: Bagels

Chive and onion cream cheese is a bagel shop favorite, and this version is no different. Whipped cream cheese, fresh chives, and minced onion make this cream cheese shmear perfect for savory bagel lovers. While a plain bagel is all you really need for this spread, it is extremely versatile! If you like smoked salmon, or lox, this cream cheese is the perfect accompaniment. It is also delicious on toasted whole-grain bread or as a spread for deli meat sandwiches. Additionally, it can be dolloped on top of a cheese omelet or scrambled eggs.

YIELDS 1 CUP, 2 TABLESPOONS PER SERVING

8 ounces whipped cream cheese
3 tablespoons fresh minced chives
2 tablespoons dehydrated minced onion
1/8 teaspoon sea salt

In a medium bowl, add all ingredients and fold to combine. Transfer to an airtight container and refrigerate 4 hours before serving. Store up to 5 days in the refrigerator.

Freeze-Dried Herbs

If you are looking for the flavor of fresh herbs without having to buy, store, and use up the herbs before they go bad, consider buying freeze-dried herbs. You can find them in most produce departments, and they can be used in the same amounts as fresh herbs. If swapping for dry herbs, use twice the amount called for in the recipe.

EINSTEIN BROS. BAGELS REDUCED FAT GARDEN VEGGIE SHMEAR

Typically Served With: Bagels

Is there a breakfast combo more iconic than bagels and cream cheese? The founders of Einstein Bros. Bagels are willing to bet there isn't! Opened in 1995, Einstein Bros. Bagels quickly became known as a place for innovative bagels, bagel sandwiches, and gourmet cream cheese shmears that range from sweet to savory. This version is one of the most popular of the savory shmears, packed with finely minced vegetables folded into fluffy whipped cream cheese. Be delicate when mixing in the vegetables to keep the cream cheese light and fluffy.

YIELDS 1 CUP, 2 TABLESPOONS PER SERVING

8 ounces whipped cream cheese
2 tablespoons minced carrot
2 tablespoons minced red bell pepper
1 tablespoon minced celery
1 tablespoon minced sweet onion
1 tablespoon minced green onion, green part only
1/8 teaspoon ground black pepper
1/8 teaspoon sea salt

In a medium bowl, add all ingredients and fold to combine. Transfer to an airtight container and refrigerate 4 hours before serving. Store up to 5 days in the refrigerator.

Just Whip It!

Want to make your own whipped cream cheese at home? Add 1 (8-ounce) block room temperature cream cheese into a medium bowl with a hand mixer or into the bowl of a stand mixer with the whip attachment. Beat on medium speed 1 minute, then increase speed to high and slowly drizzle in 1 tablespoon whole milk. Beat until as fluffy as you like, at least 2 minutes.

EINSTEIN BROS. BAGELS REDUCED FAT HONEY ALMOND SHMEAR

Typically Served With: Bagels

Sweet and crunchy, Einstein Bros. Bagels Reduced Fat Honey Almond Shmear is for those who like a sweet treat in the morning. This sweet shmear has a devoted following, and people share their favorite bagels to enjoy with it online—one of the most popular combinations is Reduced Fat Honey Almond Shmear and Cinnamon Raisin Bagel. To toast the almonds, add them to a dry skillet over medium-low heat and cook 3 minutes or until the almonds just start to toast, then remove the pan from the heat and continue to stir 15 seconds in the warm pan.

YIELDS 1 CUP, 2 TABLESPOONS PER SERVING

8 ounces whipped cream cheese
1/4 cup chopped toasted slivered almonds
2 tablespoons honey
1 tablespoon confectioners' sugar

In a medium bowl, add all ingredients and fold to combine. Transfer to an airtight container and refrigerate 4 hours before serving. Store up to 5 days in the refrigerator.

IN-N-OUT BURGER ANIMAL STYLE SPREAD

Typically Served With: Double-Double Animal Style Burger

If you are a fan of In-N-Out, you are most likely aware of their not really all that secret menu. The California-based burger chain is well-known for its fresh signature burgers and fries, but what people really love is customizing their burgers with "secret" hacks. One of the most popular is ordering their fries and burgers Animal Style. This adds cheese, grilled onions, and a creamy Thousand Island–style sauce, or (as they call it) spread. The spread makes this special, and In-N-Out customers post their own versions and order extra spread for using in mukbang videos.

YIELDS 1 CUP, 2 TABLESPOONS PER SERVING

3/4 cup mayonnaise
1/4 cup ketchup
3 tablespoons sweet pickle relish
1 teaspoon granulated sugar
1 teaspoon white vinegar

Whisk all ingredients together in a medium bowl. Transfer to an airtight container and refrigerate 4 hours before serving. Store up to 7 days in the refrigerator.

IN-N-OUT BURGER ANIMAL STYLE SPREAD

JIMMY JOHN'S KICKIN' RANCH

Typically Served As: Sandwich Spread

In 2024, fans of Jimmy John's Kickin' Ranch were devastated to learn it had been pulled from the menu. After pushback that included a petition and, from one fan, a bumper sticker that read in part, "I'm crying because I just found out Jimmy John's is discontinuing Kickin' Ranch," the chain brought it back in 2025! Lovers of Kickin' Ranch say it is so good that it can be eaten by the spoonful. In January 2025, Jimmy John's introduced a larger-format Kickin' Ranch "Soup," which is a 6-ounce container of the sauce. While they note it could be eaten as a soup, it is good for dunking sandwiches too.

YIELDS 1½ CUPS, 2 TABLESPOONS PER SERVING

½ cup buttermilk
2 pickled cherry peppers
1 tablespoon cherry pepper brine
1 cup mayonnaise
1 tablespoon dry buttermilk ranch dressing mix, such as Hidden Valley
¼ teaspoon garlic powder

1. In a blender, add buttermilk, cherry peppers, and cherry pepper brine. Purée 30 seconds or until smooth. Add remaining ingredients and purée 30 more seconds or until fully combined.
2. Transfer to an airtight container and refrigerate 4 hours before serving. Store up to 7 days in the refrigerator.

Is there Really a Jimmy John?

Yes! The chain was founded by Jimmy John Liautaud, who opened his first store in 1983 in Charleston, Illinois. Today, Jimmy is still a partial owner of the company and plays an active role as an adviser. Jimmy is a philanthropist, frequently donating money to schools and charities.

MCDONALD'S BIG MAC SAUCE

Typically Served With: Big Mac

Is there a burger sauce more popular, beloved, or widely imitated than Big Mac Sauce? Probably not! The sauce is a well-balanced combination of mayonnaise, relish, onion, and spices—but surprisingly it does not contain any ketchup! McDonald's knows how much their fans love the sauce and will occasionally tease them with special editions. For a limited time in 2023, for example, they offered tubs Big Mac Sauce lovers could use for dunking nuggets, fries, and burgers. Back in 2017, ten thousand bottles of the sauce were given away to lucky US customers, and in Canada, McDonald's sold bottles of Big Mac Sauce in retail stores.

YIELDS 1 CUP, 2 TABLESPOONS PER SERVING

3/4 cup mayonnaise
3 tablespoons sweet pickle relish
1 tablespoon grated yellow onion
1 tablespoon yellow mustard
3/4 teaspoon white vinegar
3/4 teaspoon paprika
1/4 teaspoon onion powder
1/4 teaspoon sea salt
1/4 teaspoon garlic powder

Whisk all ingredients together in a medium bowl. Transfer to an airtight container and refrigerate 4 hours before serving. Store up to 7 days in the refrigerator.

How Much Would You Pay?

When McDonald's has offered Big Mac Sauce in bottles and containers, such as the dip cups they offered in participating restaurants, some enterprising fans saw a moneymaking opportunity. Secondary market resale prices for bottles of sauce sold for hundreds of dollars, and some resellers sold sauce dip cups for even more!

MCDONALD'S BIG MAC SAUCE

RED ROBIN CAMPFIRE MAYO SAUCE

Typically Served With: Tavern Haystack Double Burger

Fans of the Red Robin Tavern Haystack Double know that the magic of that burger is the sweet and smoky sauce called Campfire Mayo. It is a sweet and spicy mix of mayonnaise, barbecue sauce, and spices. Red Robin offers this on burgers or as a side for dipping, and you can even buy it by the bottle on their catering menu. This version makes enough for burger night with extra for dipping fries and onion rings. This recipe is best made with a sweet barbecue sauce, Sweet Baby Ray's being the best option for the job.

YIELDS 1 CUP, 2 TABLESPOONS PER SERVING

2/3 cup mayonnaise
1/3 cup barbecue sauce, such as Sweet Baby Ray's
1/2 teaspoon dried chipotle powder
1/4 teaspoon smoked paprika
1/4 teaspoon lemon juice

Whisk all ingredients together in a medium bowl. Transfer to an airtight container and refrigerate 4 hours before serving. Store up to 7 days in the refrigerator.

RED ROBIN WHISKEY RIVER BBQ SAUCE

Typically Served With: Whiskey River BBQ Burger

Red Robin prides itself on making gourmet burgers with bold flavors and inventive toppings. One of those toppings is their famous Whiskey River BBQ Sauce. This fan favorite sauce is tangy and sweet, with a smooth, mellow whiskey flavor. It is so popular that the sauce is found on multiple items on the Red Robin menu. You can find it on the Whiskey River BBQ Chicken Wrap, the Whiskey River BBQ Chicken Sandwich, the Southern Charm Burger, and the Whiskey River BBQ Burger. For a burger restaurant, that's a lot of BBQ!

YIELDS 3 CUPS, 3 TABLESPOONS PER SERVING

2 cups ketchup
1/2 cup packed dark brown sugar
1/4 cup bourbon whiskey
1/4 cup apple cider vinegar
1/4 cup tomato paste
2 tablespoons Worcestershire sauce
1 tablespoon liquid smoke
1 tablespoon yellow mustard
1 teaspoon onion powder
1 teaspoon garlic powder
1/2 teaspoon ground black pepper
1/4 teaspoon salt
1/4 teaspoon hot pepper sauce, such as Tabasco

1. In a 2-quart saucepan over medium heat, add all ingredients and whisk well to combine. Bring to a boil, then reduce heat to low and simmer 20 minutes or until sauce is thick enough to coat a spoon. Serve warm or at room temperature.
2. Transfer leftover sauce to an airtight container and refrigerate. Store up to 7 days in the refrigerator.

The Red, Red Robin

Red Robin originated in Seattle, Washington, during the 1940s. Founder Samuel Caston reportedly loved the song "When the Red, Red, Robin (Comes Bob, Bob, Bobbin' Along)" and named the restaurant Sam's Red Robin Tavern. In 1969, when the restaurant was purchased by Gerry Kingen, the "Sam" and "Tavern" were dropped, making it simply "Red Robin."

SHAKE SHACK SAUCE

Typically Served With: ShackBurger

Most secret burger sauces give you a hint as to what is inside—small chunks of pickles or onion usually give away some of the flavorings. Shake Shack Sauce is sweet and tangy, with a hit of heat and another flavor that is a bit more elusive. Turns out that the flavor is dill pickle! Shake Shack purées dill pickle directly into the sauce, adding a tangy brightness and making it completely unlike any other chain's burger or sandwich sauce. This sauce benefits from chilling time. So make this at least 4 hours ahead, but 1 day ahead is even better!

YIELDS 1 CUP, 2 TABLESPOONS PER SERVING

½ cup mayonnaise
2 tablespoons finely chopped dill pickle
1 tablespoon ketchup
1 tablespoon yellow mustard
1 teaspoon dill pickle brine
¼ teaspoon onion powder
¼ teaspoon garlic powder
¼ teaspoon paprika
⅛ teaspoon cayenne pepper

1. Place all ingredients in a blender and purée until smooth, about 1 minute, stopping midway to scrape down sides of blender.
2. Transfer to an airtight container and refrigerate 4 hours before serving. Store up to 5 days in the refrigerator.

Mukbang

Directly translated from Korean, "mukbang" means "eating broadcast," and since the 2010s, it has become one of the most popular Internet trends. People most often livestream themselves eating everything from single meals to entire restaurant menus while talking to the people commenting in the chat, and they will post clips to popular apps like TikTok and Instagram.

SONIC CHILI

Typically Served With: Chili Cheese Coney

Nothing quite beats a hot dog smothered in beefy chili and shredded cheese, does it? Or perhaps on a basket of fries or Tater Tots? Sonic has perfected a chili recipe that you can enjoy on their Chili Cheese Coney, Fritos Chili Cheese Wrap, Chili Cheese Groovy Fries, or Chili Cheese Tots. You can also add it to any burger or sandwich on their menu for an additional charge. The original Sonic Chili does not contain beans, but if you enjoy beans in your chili, add 1 (15-ounce) can of rinsed and drained kidney beans to the pot for the last 10 minutes of cooking.

YIELDS 4 CUPS, 1/2 CUP PER SERVING

1 tablespoon vegetable oil
1 pound 90/10 lean ground beef
1 small white onion, peeled and finely chopped
2 tablespoons finely minced garlic
1 (6-ounce) can tomato paste
2 tablespoons chili powder
2 teaspoons cumin
1 teaspoon sea salt
1 teaspoon ground black pepper
1 teaspoon cayenne pepper
2 cups beef broth

1. In a deep-sided Dutch oven over medium heat, add oil. Once oil is hot and simmering, add ground beef. Cook, crumbling well, until no pink remains, about 8 minutes.
2. Add onion and cook until onion is tender, about 5 minutes, then add garlic and tomato paste and cook 2 minutes or until tomato paste is darker in color, then stir in chili powder, cumin, salt, black pepper, and cayenne pepper and cook until spices are fragrant, about 30 seconds.
3. Stir in broth, scraping bottom of pot well to release any brown bits. Bring mixture to a boil, then reduce heat to low, cover with a lid, and simmer 30 minutes, stirring occasionally.
4. Remove lid and continue to simmer 20–30 minutes until chili is thickened to your preference. Serve immediately.

SONIC SMASHER SAUCE

Typically Served With: Double Sonic Smasher

As competition heats up in the fast-food burger market, it makes sense that chains are aiming to give customers a high-end experience with reasonable prices. Enter the Double Sonic Smasher made with two hand-smashed-to-order all-Angus-beef patties, two slices of melted American cheese, a soft potato bread bun, dill pickles, chopped onions, and the new Sonic Smasher Sauce. The sauce, introduced along with the burger in the summer of 2024, is the perfect creamy yet tangy complement to the savory meat and lightly sweet bun, and it replaced the Sonic Signature Sauce. This sauce is also good on grilled or crispy chicken sandwiches or as a dip for chicken nuggets.

YIELDS 1 CUP, 2 TABLESPOONS PER SERVING

½ cup mayonnaise
1 tablespoon plus 2 teaspoons ketchup
1 tablespoon yellow mustard
1 tablespoon dill pickle brine
¼ teaspoon onion powder
¼ teaspoon garlic powder
¼ teaspoon paprika

Whisk all ingredients together in a medium bowl. Transfer to an airtight container and refrigerate 4 hours before serving. Store up to 7 days in the refrigerator.

Sonic Saucy Changes

Aside from adding Smasher Sauce, Sonic has made other changes to their sauces. They added Groovy Sauce (Chapter 7) as a dipping sauce for their Groovy Fries. They also changed from offering mustard and ketchup as the default burger sauces to ketchup and mayonnaise. Mustard is available by special request.

SUBWAY BAJA CHIPOTLE SAUCE

Typically Served With: Oven-Roasted Turkey Sub

In 2022, Subway refreshed its menu with the introduction of the Subway Series, featuring higher-quality ingredients and updated flavors. They added new offerings, including a line of signature sandwiches, premium toppings like fresh mozzarella, and better-quality guacamole, and they updated some of their signature sauces. One change was updating their Chipotle Southwest Sauce to Baja Chipotle Sauce, which has a stronger chipotle flavor and a bit more zing from tangy buttermilk and a bit of vinegar. In 2025, Subway developed two limited-time-only subs around the Baja Chipotle Sauce: the Baja Chipotle Turkey and Baja Chipotle Chicken.

YIELDS 1¼ CUPS, 2 TABLESPOONS PER SERVING

½ cup sour cream
¼ cup buttermilk
¼ cup mayonnaise
2 tablespoons chipotle in adobo, mashed into a paste
1 tablespoon white vinegar
1 teaspoon onion powder
½ teaspoon dried dill
½ teaspoon garlic powder
¼ teaspoon ground black pepper
¼ teaspoon sea salt
¼ teaspoon paprika

Whisk all ingredients together in a medium bowl. Transfer to an airtight container and refrigerate 4 hours before serving. Store up to 7 days in the refrigerator.

SUBWAY BAJA CHIPOTLE SAUCE

SUBWAY ROASTED GARLIC AIOLI

Typically Served As: Sandwich Spread

Subway has a lineup of signature sauces that customers can use to liven up the chain's sandwich creations. One of the most popular is the Roasted Garlic Aioli. This Mediterranean-inspired sauce has roasted garlic and spices with a hint of lemon flavor to make it rich yet refreshing. You can add as much or as little roasted garlic to this sauce as you like, so feel free to add as many cloves as you want. For every 2 cloves added, be sure to add ½ teaspoon of olive oil so they roast properly.

YIELDS 1 CUP, 2 TABLESPOONS PER SERVING

4 cloves garlic
1 teaspoon olive oil
1 cup mayonnaise
2 teaspoons lemon juice
½ teaspoon sugar
¼ teaspoon ground black pepper
¼ teaspoon sea salt

1. Preheat oven to 375°F.
2. On a 6-inch piece of aluminum foil, add garlic cloves and oil. Toss cloves to coat in oil, then wrap tightly in foil. Bake in oven 45–55 minutes until cloves are golden brown and very tender. Remove from oven, unwrap, and cool.
3. In a food processor, add garlic along with remaining ingredients and pulse to combine, about 15 pulses.
4. Transfer to an airtight container and refrigerate 4 hours before serving. Store up to 5 days in the refrigerator.

What Is Aioli?

A true aioli is made from pounding garlic into a fine paste, adding a bit of lemon juice, then slowly adding olive oil a tablespoon at a time while mashing to make a creamy, thick sauce. While some restaurants will make aioli this way, it is much easier to use mayonnaise and flavor it with garlic.

SUBWAY SWEET ONION TERIYAKI

Typically Served With: All-Pro Sweet Onion Chicken Teriyaki Sandwich

In 2002, Subway introduced what would become one of its most popular signature sauces of all time. They also created a line of gourmet-inspired sandwiches with an advertised 6 grams of fat or less per sub. The new line included the Sweet Onion Chicken Teriyaki sub, which was an immediate success! The sub had teriyaki-glazed white meat chicken and included a new sauce: Sweet Onion Teriyaki. This sauce was advertised as fat-free but flavor packed. Customers loved this new sauce and started adding it to other subs on the menu. The sauce is an excellent marinade and can also be used as a stir-fry sauce or for tossing vegetables for a sheet pan dinner.

YIELDS 1 CUP, 2 TABLESPOONS PER SERVING

½ cup light corn syrup
2 tablespoons rice vinegar
1 tablespoon light soy sauce
1 tablespoon grated yellow onion
1 tablespoon water
1 teaspoon tomato paste
2 teaspoons Dijon mustard
1 teaspoon dry mustard powder
1 teaspoon minced dehydrated onion
1 teaspoon poppy seeds
1 teaspoon sesame seeds
⅛ teaspoon ground ginger
⅛ teaspoon paprika

1. In a 1-quart pan over medium heat, combine all ingredients and whisk well. Bring to a boil, about 5 minutes, then remove from heat and cool to room temperature.
2. Transfer to an airtight container and refrigerate 4 hours before serving. Store up to 7 days in the refrigerator.

Make It in a Flash

To make this sauce in a hurry, you can combine ¾ cup prepared teriyaki sauce, such as Kikkoman, with the recipe ingredients starting with tomato paste and whisk until smooth. Transfer to an airtight container and refrigerate 4 hours before serving. Store up to 7 days in the refrigerator.

CHAPTER 5

INTO THE SEA: SEAFOOD SAUCES

Sizzling fried shrimp, savory boiled seafood, and teppanyaki-style seafood are all tasty, but they have one thing in common that takes them over the top, and that is a delicious sauce! Seafood sauces come in a variety of flavors and textures and can be mild and sweet to bold and spicy. This chapter has a variety of recipes for seafood dips and dressings that span this range. For fried seafood, you will find classics like Long John Silver's Cocktail Sauce and Red Lobster Tartar Sauce. There are bold and spicy sauces for boiled seafood like The Boiling Crab The Whole Sha-Bang! and G's Sea-Sauce. There are sweeter seafood sauces like Bubba Gump Shrimp Co. Maker's Mark Bourbon Sauce and Red Lobster Piña Colada Sauce, which are perfect for your favorite fried and boiled shrimp. There are also popular imitation Asian sauces like Benihana Yum Yum Sauce and Ginger Sauce. Some seafood sauces are so popular that guests will order them by the pint to enjoy at home! With the recipes in this chapter, you can skip the restaurant and make as much of your favorite sauces as you like in the comfort of your own home.

BENIHANA GINGER SAUCE

Typically Served With: Hibachi Entrées

In 1964 the first Benihana in the United States was opened in New York City by Hiroaki "Rocky" Aoki, the son of Yunosuke Aoki, who had established his own Benihana in Tokyo in the 1940s after the end of World War II. Hiroaki aimed to create an exciting teppanyaki dining experience for American customers combining a meal with an entertaining show. The teppanyaki chefs provided both the food and the show, entertaining guests with jokes, knife tricks, and spatula spins and flips while they cooked at the grill. The concept took off after a glowing review in 1965 in the *New York Herald Tribune*, and today the chain has over seventy locations in North, South, and Central America and the Caribbean. This light sauce has a kick from fresh ginger and lemon. The refreshing taste pairs well with grilled meat and seafood.

YIELDS 2 CUPS, 1/4 CUP PER SERVING

1 medium yellow onion, peeled and sliced
2-inch piece fresh ginger, peeled and roughly chopped
3/4 cup light soy sauce
1/4 cup rice vinegar
1/4 cup lemon juice
1 tablespoon lemon zest
1 tablespoon granulated sugar

1. Place all ingredients in a blender and purée on high until smooth, about 1 minute.
2. Transfer to an airtight container and refrigerate 4 hours before serving. Store up to 4 days in the refrigerator. Stir well before serving.

A Bit of Benihana History

The first Benihana opened in Tokyo as a coffee shop in 1947, and in 1950 a restaurant was added on the floor above. In 1955, Benihana's founder, Yunosuke Aoki, opened a second restaurant across the street. Renovated and renamed Benihana Bekkan in 1964, this venture included a a teppanyaki restaurant. In 1956, a Benihana location opened in the Tokyo neighborhood of Ginza. This location continued to operate until 1997, when the building was demolished to make way for new building construction.

BENIHANA YUM YUM SAUCE

Typically Served With: Hibachi Shrimp

Benihana Yum Yum Sauce is among the most popular items they offer. The lightly pink sauce is perfect for dipping meats and seafood fresh off the grill. While many assume the sauce is Japanese in origin, that does not appear to be the case. Oliver Whang, reporting for NPR in 2019, noted that multiple experts on Japanese cuisine had never heard of the condiment, so it appears to be an American invention. Yum Yum Sauce is beloved by fans and often duplicated by other hibachi/teppanyaki restaurants, but nothing beats the Benihana original, except maybe this copycat version!

YIELDS 1¼ CUPS, 2 TABLESPOONS PER SERVING

1 cup mayonnaise
2 tablespoons water
1 tablespoon unsalted butter, melted
2 teaspoons rice vinegar
2 teaspoons tomato paste
1 teaspoon granulated sugar
½ teaspoon paprika
¼ teaspoon garlic powder
¼ teaspoon onion powder
⅛ teaspoon cayenne pepper

Whisk all ingredients together in a medium bowl. Transfer to an airtight container and refrigerate 4 hours before serving. Store up to 7 days in the refrigerator.

A Sauce by Any Other Name

Yum Yum Sauce, so named because it is so yummy, is often duplicated by the competition and goes by different names at different restaurants. You may see it called shrimp sauce, white sauce, seafood sauce, or pink sauce, but the original Yum Yum Sauce is only found at Benihana.

THE BOILING CRAB GARLIC BUTTER

Typically Served With: Seafood Boils

Garlic lovers will be thrilled with this spiced garlic butter! You can serve it as a dipping sauce, or you can use it for tossing boiled seafood, making it very versatile. This sauce features plenty of garlic along with a bit of lemon, seafood seasoning, and a little brown sugar to balance the flavors. It has lots of delicious fresh garlic, which means you should take care to safely cool and store this sauce if you have any leftovers to avoid harmful bacteria growth. If you will not be using up the sauce within 3 days, consider freezing it for longer storage.

YIELDS 1 CUP, 2 TABLESPOONS PER SERVING

1 cup unsalted butter
8 cloves garlic, peeled and minced
1 tablespoon fresh lemon juice
1 tablespoon seafood seasoning, such as Old Bay
2 teaspoons packed light brown sugar
½ teaspoon hot pepper sauce, such as Tabasco
½ teaspoon sea salt

1. In a 1-quart saucepan over medium heat, add butter. Once butter is melted, add remaining ingredients and cook 3 minutes or until garlic is tender and spices are fragrant. Remove from heat and cool 5 minutes before serving or tossing with boiled seafood.
2. Transfer leftover sauce to an airtight container and refrigerate. Store up to 3 days in the refrigerator. Reheat sauce in the microwave in 30-second intervals or until hot and steamy.

The Boiling Crab, a Love Story

According to The Boiling Crab's website, founders Yo'Daddy (Sinh Nguyen) and Yo'Mama (Dada Ngo) met in Seadrift, Texas, while Yo'Daddy was working as a crabber and fisherman. They fell in love and, with Yo'Mama's flair for hospitality, opened their first location in 2004 in Garden Grove, California. Today, The Boiling Crab has thirty locations serving "the best tail in town"!

THE BOILING CRAB G'S SEA-SAUCE

Typically Served With: Fried Oysters

Sweet, spicy, and a little tangy, G's Sea-Sauce is perfect for dipping boiled and fried seafood and fish. The Boiling Crab bills the sauce as having a kick and being perfect for dipping. They have featured their G's Sea-Sauce on social media, along with their fried and fresh oysters. In one video a plump fried oyster is dunked into the sauce, leaving it glossy red and irresistible looking! In another, a fresh oyster is smothered in a spoonful of the spicy condiment.

YIELDS 3/4 CUP, 2 TABLESPOONS PER SERVING

1/4 cup ketchup
1/4 cup hot pepper sauce, such as Tabasco
3 tablespoons honey
1 teaspoon seafood seasoning, such as Old Bay
1/2 teaspoon garlic powder
1/2 teaspoon ground black pepper

Whisk all ingredients together in a medium bowl. Transfer to an airtight container and refrigerate 4 hours before serving. Store up to 5 days in the refrigerator.

THE BOILING CRAB G'S SEA-SAUCE

THE BOILING CRAB RAJUN CAJUN

Typically Served With: Seafood Boils

The Boiling Crab is a Cajun-style restaurant, so it makes sense that one of their signature seafood boil sauces would be Cajun flavored. This recipe combines butter and Cajun spices along with a bit of lemon and Worcestershire sauce to make the perfect savory seafood boil. This sauce is excellent for tossing or serving as a dip for any seafood, but it is particularly delicious on boiled crawfish and shrimp! For those who are not seafood lovers, it is also wonderful for tossing cooked andouille sausage, boiled new potatoes and corn, or any roasted or steamed vegetables.

YIELDS 1 CUP, 2 TABLESPOONS PER SERVING

1 cup unsalted butter
1/4 cup Cajun seasoning, such as Tony Chachere's Original Creole Seasoning
1 tablespoon smoked paprika
1 tablespoon fresh lemon juice
1 teaspoon Worcestershire sauce

1. In a 1-quart saucepan over medium heat, add butter. Once butter is melted, add remaining ingredients and cook 2–3 minutes until spices are fragrant. Remove from heat and cool 5 minutes before serving or tossing with boiled seafood.
2. Transfer leftover sauce to an airtight container and refrigerate. Store up to 4 days in the refrigerator. Reheat sauce in the microwave in 30-second intervals or until hot and steamy.

THE BOILING CRAB THE WHOLE SHA-BANG!

Typically Served With: Seafood Boils

Can't decide between Garlic Butter, Rajun Cajun, or Lemon Pepper for your seafood boil? With The Whole Sha-Bang! sauce from The Boiling Crab, you don't have to! This sauce is the perfect blend of rich, zippy, and spicy and can be used for tossing freshly boiled or steamed seafood or dipping steamed, baked, or grilled seafood. It is also good for dipping or coating crispy fried chicken tenders or using as a dip for fries or onion rings. This sauce is The Boiling Crab's signature and is so popular, they trademarked the name!

YIELDS 1 CUP, 2 TABLESPOONS PER SERVING

1 cup unsalted butter
6 cloves garlic, peeled and minced
1 tablespoon fresh lemon juice
1 tablespoon seafood seasoning, such as Old Bay
1 tablespoon Cajun seasoning, such as Tony Chachere's Original Creole Seasoning
1 tablespoon paprika
1 tablespoon lemon pepper
1 tablespoon hot pepper sauce, such as Tabasco
2 teaspoons packed light brown sugar

1. In a 1-quart saucepan over medium heat, add butter. Once butter is melted, add remaining ingredients and cook 2–3 minutes until garlic is tender and spices are fragrant. Remove from heat and cool 5 minutes before serving or tossing with boiled seafood.
2. Transfer leftover sauce to an airtight container and refrigerate. Store up to 4 days in the refrigerator. Reheat sauce in the microwave in 30-second intervals or until hot and steamy.

Seafood Feasts

Modern seafood boils originated in eighteenth-century Louisiana when Cajun and creole food traditions merged, and large pots of spiced, buttery seafood were served up for friends, family, and neighbors. The concept evolved from backyards to restaurants, where seafood is still served directly in the center of the table so everyone can share!

BONEFISH GRILL IMPERIAL DIP

Typically Served With: Seasoned Tortilla Chips

This popular dip at Bonefish Grill is packed with three types of seafood, three types of gooey cheese, and plenty of delicious seasonings. It's so popular that it consistently ranks as one of the chain's bestselling menu items! Enjoy it with seasoned tortilla chips like they serve it at Bonefish Grill by arranging 6 ounces of tortilla chips on a baking sheet, spraying lightly with nonstick cooking spray, and sprinkling evenly with 1 teaspoon of Old Bay seasoning, then baking at 375°F 6–8 minutes until chips are warm. You can make this dip up to the point of baking, cover, and refrigerate a day in advance.

SERVES 6

1 teaspoon vegetable oil
1/2 cup bay scallops
1/2 pound 50–60 count raw shrimp, peeled and deveined, roughly chopped
2 tablespoons finely minced yellow onion
1 clove garlic, peeled and minced
1 large egg, beaten
1/2 cup mayonnaise
1/4 cup shredded whole milk mozzarella
1/4 cup shredded Gruyère cheese
1/4 cup freshly grated Parmesan cheese, divided
1/2 teaspoon fresh lemon juice
1/2 teaspoon Worcestershire sauce
1/2 teaspoon Old Bay seasoning
1/2 teaspoon dry mustard
1/4 teaspoon cayenne pepper
1/4 teaspoon sea salt
8 ounces jumbo lump crabmeat
1 tablespoon unsalted butter, melted
1/3 cup panko bread crumbs

1. Preheat oven to 375°F and spray an 8-inch baking dish with nonstick cooking spray.
2. In a 10-inch nonstick skillet over medium heat, add oil. Once oil is hot, add scallops, shrimp, and onion and sauté until just cooked through, about 1 minute. Add garlic and cook 30 seconds or until very fragrant. Remove from pan and cool 10 minutes.
3. In a medium bowl, combine egg, mayonnaise, mozzarella, Gruyère, 2 tablespoons Parmesan, lemon juice, Worcestershire sauce, Old Bay, mustard, cayenne pepper, and salt and mix until well combined. Fold in cooked crabmeat and scallop and shrimp mixture. Spread evenly into prepared baking dish.
4. In a small bowl, combine melted butter and panko and toss to coat. Stir in remaining Parmesan, then sprinkle mixture evenly over dip.
5. Bake 20–25 minutes until dip is bubbling hot around edges and topping is golden brown. Cool 3 minutes before serving.

BONEFISH GRILL LEMON BUTTER SAUCE

Typically Served With: Parmesan-Crusted Rainbow Trout

Bonefish Grill serves a dreamy, rich lemon butter sauce that perfectly accompanies their Parmesan-Crusted Rainbow Trout or any grilled fish they offer. It is a lemony take on beurre blanc, a white butter sauce, invented in France by chef Clémence Lefeuvre. As the story goes, she was making a béarnaise sauce and forgot to add the tarragon and egg yolk, and the resulting sauce was silky and light in texture but with a rich, buttery flavor. The Bonefish Grill version swaps the traditional vinegar for lemon juice, making it bright, rich, and perfect for your favorite fish dishes!

SERVES 4

1 cup dry white wine
1/4 cup lemon juice
2 tablespoons minced shallots
1/2 clove garlic, peeled and minced
1 tablespoon heavy whipping cream
12 tablespoons unsalted butter, cubed and chilled
1/4 teaspoon sea salt

1. In a 1-quart saucepan over medium heat, add wine, lemon juice, shallots, and garlic. Bring to a boil, then reduce heat to medium-low and simmer until reduced to 2 tablespoons, about 15 minutes.
2. Reduce heat to low and stir in cream, then whisk in butter 1 or 2 cubes at a time, making sure the previous butter is melted before adding more. After every other addition of butter, move the pan off the heat to keep the sauce from getting too warm. When you have 4 or 5 cubes left, remove pot from heat and continue to whisk in cubes until sauce is smooth and glossy. Whisk in salt. Serve immediately.

Other Uses

This Lemon Butter Sauce is likely to become a mealtime favorite at your house when you add it to dishes like grilled or baked chicken or grilled or sautéed shrimp, or drizzle it over roasted vegetables or pan-fried pork chops. For an herby touch, add 1 teaspoon fresh chopped dill or chives when you add the wine.

BUBBA GUMP SHRIMP CO. MAKER'S MARK BOURBON SAUCE

Typically Served With: Maker's Mark Salmon

This sweet and sticky sauce is served as a dipping sauce for many menu items, but it is best loved when served with Maker's Mark Salmon. This dish is a flame-grilled salmon fillet served with rice and broccoli and a side of this sauce for drizzling and dipping. The sauce can also be used as a glaze while grilling, pan searing, or roasting for a shiny coating and golden brown color. For those avoiding alcohol, the bourbon can be replaced with an equal amount of apple cider; just reduce the amount of brown sugar to 3 tablespoons.

SERVES 4

1/2 cup Maker's Mark Kentucky Straight Bourbon
1/4 cup packed light brown sugar
1 tablespoon red wine vinegar
1 teaspoon Worcestershire sauce
1/4 teaspoon onion powder
2 teaspoons cornstarch
2 teaspoons water

1. In a 1-quart saucepan over medium heat, add bourbon. Bring to a boil, then reduce heat to low and simmer 5 minutes. Add in brown sugar, vinegar, Worcestershire sauce, and onion powder and whisk well to combine. Continue to simmer 3–4 minutes until sauce has reduced by 1/4.
2. Increase heat to medium and bring sauce to a boil. Once boiling, combine cornstarch and water in a small bowl and then whisk into boiling sauce. Cook 15 seconds, then remove from heat. Serve hot.

BUBBA GUMP SHRIMP CO. REMOULADE SAUCE

Typically Served With: Forrest's Seafood Feast

Bubba Gump Shrimp Co. sells, as the name implies, shrimp dishes, as well as other seafood meals and Southern comfort food dishes. They opened in 1996 in Monterey, California, after founder Anthony Zolezzi purchased the rights to the name in 1995. Shrimp, cooked in almost any way you can imagine, is one of the big sellers, and fans of the chain love the Remoulade Sauce to dip the shrimp in. You can adjust the spice in this sauce by adding more or less hot pepper sauce, or feel free to add 1/8–1/4 teaspoon cayenne pepper for an extra kick!

YIELDS 1 1/4 CUPS, 3 TABLESPOONS PER SERVING

1 cup mayonnaise
2 tablespoons creole mustard
1 teaspoon prepared horseradish
1/2 teaspoon Worcestershire sauce
1/2 teaspoon paprika
1/2 teaspoon onion powder
1/4 teaspoon garlic powder
1/4 teaspoon hot pepper sauce, such as Tabasco

Whisk all ingredients together in a medium bowl. Transfer to an airtight container and refrigerate 4 hours before serving. Store up to 5 days in the refrigerator.

A Box O' Chocolates

Bubba Gump Seafood Co. leans hard into movie nostalgia. The menu contains items named for characters in the movie *Forrest Gump*, such as Jenny's Salmon & Shrimp and Forrest's Seafood Feast. For dessert, you can drop into the gift shop for a Box O' Chocolates, a mix of truffles and English toffee covered in milk and dark chocolate.

BUBBA GUMP SHRIMP CO. REMOULADE SAUCE

CARRABBA'S ITALIAN GRILL RICARDO SAUCE

Typically Served With: Calamari

This popular dipping sauce is served with Carrabba's crisp fried Calamari appetizer along with a side of marinara sauce. The rich, buttery flavor, with a hint of tang from lemon and pepperoncino peppers, complements fried calamari or any fried seafood. The Ricardo Sauce was briefly removed from the menu, but fans made it known they wanted it back, and in 2021 it was brought back for good! This sauce is a butter emulsion like beurre blanc, so take care to keep it from getting too warm and splitting while whisking in the butter.

SERVES 2

2 tablespoons clarified butter
2 tablespoons finely chopped red bell pepper
2 tablespoons finely chopped yellow onion
2 cloves garlic, peeled and minced
3 tablespoons pickled pepperoncino pepper rings
1/4 cup fresh lemon juice
3 tablespoons dry white wine
1 tablespoon heavy whipping cream
2 tablespoons unsalted butter, cubed and chilled
1/2 teaspoon sea salt
1/4 teaspoon crushed red pepper flakes

1. In a 1-quart saucepan over medium heat, add clarified butter. Once butter is hot, add bell pepper, onion, and garlic and sauté 1 minute. Add pepper rings, lemon juice, and wine and stir well. Bring to a boil, then reduce heat to medium-low and simmer until reduced to 2 tablespoons, about 10 minutes.
2. Reduce heat to low and stir in cream, then whisk in butter 1 or 2 cubes at a time, making sure the previous butter is melted before adding more. After every other addition of butter, move the pan off the heat to keep the sauce from getting too warm. When you have 2 or 3 cubes left, remove pot from heat and continue to whisk in cubes until sauce is smooth and glossy. Whisk in salt and red pepper flakes. Serve immediately.

Adding a Touch of Cream

Beurre blanc is an emulsion of butter whisked into reduced wine and vinegar, and is notorious for splitting if it gets too hot. To help the emulsion stay stable, a touch of heavy whipping cream can be added just before the butter to keep the sauce creamy and smooth.

LONG JOHN SILVER'S COCKTAIL SAUCE

Typically Served With: Fried Shrimp

Long John Silver's is famous for fish planks, fried shrimp, and those yummy little crispy batter pieces that—let's be honest—are hard to resist. With all that seafood, it makes sense that they have their own special dipping sauces. Their Cocktail Sauce is perfect for dunking crisp fried shrimp and fish and is different from other cocktail sauces because it is milder and a bit sweeter. If you want more heat in your cocktail sauce, you can add more horseradish or 1/4–1/2 teaspoon of your favorite hot pepper sauce.

YIELDS 1 CUP, 2 TABLESPOONS PER SERVING

1 cup ketchup
1 tablespoon prepared horseradish
1 teaspoon lemon juice
1 teaspoon granulated sugar
1/2 teaspoon Worcestershire sauce
1/8 teaspoon onion powder
1/8 teaspoon garlic powder
1/8 teaspoon paprika

Whisk all ingredients together in a medium bowl. Transfer to an airtight container and refrigerate 4 hours before serving. Store up to 5 days in the refrigerator.

A Literary Name

In 1969, Jim Patterson opened the first Long John Silver's Fish & Chips in Lexington, Kentucky. Finding the right name to grab the public's attention turned out to be fairly easy. He named his restaurant after the main antagonist, Long John Silver, in Robert Lewis Stevensons' 1883 classic novel, *Treasure Island*.

MCDONALD'S TARTAR SAUCE

Typically Served With: Filet-O-Fish

The Filet-O-Fish was introduced in 1962 by franchise owner Lou Groen for McDonald's customers who did not eat meat on Fridays or during certain religious holidays. This sandwich helped boost sales on those slower traffic days and is a popular sandwich with fans today. The Filet-O-Fish is part of a viral "menu hack" sandwich called the Land, Air, and Sea Burger. This secret menu DIY sandwich combines a Filet-O-Fish plank, a Big Mac patty, and a McChicken fillet, all stacked on a bun. That's a mouthful!

YIELDS 3/4 CUP, 2 TABLESPOONS PER SERVING

1/2 cup mayonnaise
3 tablespoons dill pickle relish
2 tablespoons finely minced yellow onion
1/2 teaspoon dried parsley
1/2 teaspoon granulated sugar

Whisk all ingredients together in a medium bowl. Transfer to an airtight container and refrigerate 4 hours before serving. Store up to 5 days in the refrigerator.

Hula Burger History

McDonald's founder, Ray Kroc, wanted to provide a meatless burger option to Catholics and those abstaining from meat and came up with the Hula Burger. It was a grilled pineapple served with a slice of cheese on a burger bun. Unsurprisingly, the Hula Burger did not take off with McDonald's fans, losing out in 1962 to a competition with Filet-O-Fish, which remained on the menu.

MCDONALD'S TARTAR SAUCE

RED LOBSTER COCKTAIL SAUCE

Typically Served With: Walt's Favorite Shrimp

Red Lobster Cocktail Sauce is zesty and savory and perfect for dipping Walt's Favorite Shrimp or any fried shrimp and seafood on the menu. It is popular with Red Lobster fans, with one fan on Reddit claiming they could drink the sauce by the gallon! This recipe ups the savory flavor by adding a bit of chili sauce and white pepper. If you prefer a bit more spice, you can add ¼–⅛ teaspoon of your favorite hot pepper sauce. Alternatively, to reduce the savoriness, use ¼–½ teaspoon of granulated sugar.

YIELDS 1 CUP, 2 TABLESPOONS PER SERVING

⅓ cup ketchup
¼ cup chili sauce
1 tablespoon prepared horseradish
1 teaspoon Worcestershire sauce
1 teaspoon lemon juice
⅛ teaspoon white pepper

Whisk all ingredients together in a medium bowl. Transfer to an airtight container and refrigerate 4 hours before serving. Store up to 5 days in the refrigerator.

Walter King

Hired in 1971, Walter "Walt" King is the namesake for one of Reb Lobster's most popular dishes: Walt's Favorite Shrimp. Walt, who passed away in 2023, was one of the chain's first employees, hired in 1971 as a manager. He worked for Red Lobster for 36 years in various leadership positions.

RED LOBSTER PIÑA COLADA SAUCE

Typically Served With: Parrot Isle Jumbo Coconut Shrimp Appetizer

Most restaurants serve coconut shrimp with Thai sweet chili sauce or sweet and sour sauce, but Red Lobster has taken a more Caribbean turn with their Piña Colada Sauce. This sauce is made with finely diced pineapple, Coco Lopez Cream of Coconut (a sweetened coconut cream), and sour cream for a savory tang. The sweet and savory flavor pairs well with crisp coconut shrimp, but it can also be enjoyed with grilled white fish, fried or baked fish fingers, or even fried chicken tenders and nuggets. If you can't find Coco Lopez, you can substitute an equal amount of piña colada mixer.

YIELDS 1 CUP, 2 TABLESPOONS PER SERVING

½ cup sour cream
⅓ cup Coco Lopez Cream of Coconut
¼ cup finely diced canned pineapple
1 tablespoon powdered sugar
1 teaspoon lemon juice

Whisk all ingredients together in a medium bowl. Transfer to an airtight container and refrigerate 4 hours before serving. Store up to 5 days in the refrigerator.

RED LOBSTER TARTAR SAUCE

Typically Served With: Admiral's Feast

Red Lobster Tartar Sauce has always been a guest favorite because of the unique flavor. The addition of a little sugar, sweet pickle relish, and, uniquely, finely grated carrot make the sauce sweeter while still keeping a savory edge. In 2024, Red Lobster updated their Tartar Sauce recipe, much to the dismay of longtime customers, and received a lot of negative feedback at the restaurant and on online spaces. This recipe captures the flavor of the classic so you can enjoy that perfectly savory-sweet flavor with your favorite fish and seafood at home!

YIELDS 1¼ CUPS, 2 TABLESPOONS PER SERVING

2 tablespoons finely grated carrot
1 cup mayonnaise
3 tablespoons finely minced yellow onion
2 tablespoons sweet pickle relish
¼ teaspoon granulated sugar

Chop grated carrot until the carrot pieces are very fine. Add to a medium bowl along with remaining ingredients and whisk to combine. Transfer to an airtight container and refrigerate 4 hours before serving. Store up to 5 days in the refrigerator.

Endless Shrimp or Endless Trouble?

Many blame Red Lobster's financial struggles in recent years on their endless shrimp promotion, but other factors such as declining customer traffic, increasing costs, and financial mismanagement also played a role. With some changes and a reorganization of their debt, Red Lobster is back and ready to impress customers, but their all-you-can-eat shrimp is gone for good.

CHAPTER 6

LIGHTER FARE: SALAD DRESSINGS AND MARINADES

A salad is just a bowl of greens until you add a drizzle of dressing, and a steak or piece of chicken is nothing special without a savory marinade to amp up the flavor. In this chapter, you will find recipes to help you make restaurant salad dressings and marinades so good that you will be able to re-create your steakhouse favorites at home! Planning on Italian night at home? Why not whip up a batch of Olive Garden Italian Dressing to dress a crisp salad? Doing some barbecuing or grilling for dinner? A batch of Dickey's Barbecue Pit Coleslaw Dressing on your favorite coleslaw mix makes a delicious and fresh side, and you can pair that coleslaw with El Pollo Loco Chicken Marinade, which is the perfect marinade for the chicken you are grilling. From light lunches, sides, and main dishes, this chapter has dressings and marinades to take your food from fine to fabulous! The recipes in this chapter make dressing up any meal easy and delicious.

APPLEBEE'S NEIGHBORHOOD GRILL + BAR ORIENTAL VINAIGRETTE

Typically Served With: Applebee's Oriental Chicken Salad

Since 1980, Applebee's has been a staple in cities across America, serving tasty food and drinks. One menu staple that fans adore is the Oriental Chicken Salad. This long-time favorite salad has mixed greens, crunchy chow mein noodles, sliced almonds, your choice of crispy or grilled chicken, and a sweet and tangy dressing that fans can't get enough of! The dressing is so popular, people online have been speculating about the ingredients to find out what makes it so tasty. This recipe makes an almost exact duplicate of the restaurant version and can also be used as a dip for fried or grilled chicken.

YIELDS 1¼ CUPS, ¼ CUP PER SERVING

½ cup honey
¼ cup rice vinegar
½ cup mayonnaise
1 tablespoon Dijon mustard
½ teaspoon sesame oil

Whisk all ingredients together in a medium bowl. Use immediately or transfer to an airtight container and store up to 7 days in the refrigerator.

Evolution of the Brand

When Applebee's first opened in Decatur, Georgia, in 1980, it was called T.J. Applebee's Rx for Edibles & Elixirs. That is quite a mouthful! New owners changed the name in 1986 to the more customer-friendly Applebee's Neighborhood Grill + Bar, which is the official name of the chain. Today, most people call it simply Applebee's!

APPLEBEE'S NEIGHBORHOOD GRILL + BAR ORIENTAL VINAIGRETTE

BAHAMA BREEZE ISLAND VINAIGRETTE

Typically Served With: Salmon Tostada Salad

Bright, fresh, and with a burst of citrus, this salad dressing tastes like a Caribbean vacation in the comfort of your own kitchen! It is perfect to pair with mixed greens and fresh grilled salmon like they do at Bahama Breeze. It is also delicious on just about any salad you like and can even be used as a marinade for fresh seafood, fish, or chicken. Simply coat your protein of choice in the dressing and let it sit in the refrigerator 10 minutes for seafood and fish or up to 1 hour for chicken. Then you can cook as desired.

YIELDS 1¼ CUPS, 3 TABLESPOONS PER SERVING

⅔ cup rice vinegar
⅓ cup fresh orange juice
2 tablespoons olive oil
2 tablespoons fresh chopped cilantro
1 tablespoon Dijon mustard
1 tablespoon minced shallot
1 clove garlic, peeled and minced
1 teaspoon honey
½ teaspoon creole seasoning, such as Tony Chachere's Original Creole Seasoning

Whisk all ingredients together in a medium bowl. Use immediately or transfer to an airtight container and store up to 4 days in the refrigerator.

They Love It on TikTok

Bahama Breeze has a dedicated following on TikTok, with fans of the restaurant chain sharing copycat recipes, menu reviews, and favorite meals and drinks for their followers. Recipes you find often include Island Vinaigrette, Tropical Chicken Salad, and Jerk Chicken Pasta, with one video having almost 30,000 likes!

BOB EVANS COLONIAL DRESSING

Typically Served With: Cranberry Pecan Chicken Salad

Starting as a small diner to sell Bob Evans' homemade sausage, his restaurant chain eventually grew into a food empire with a restaurant division and a retail grocery division. In the restaurants, you will find a variety of classic comfort meals, including some tasty salads and dressings. Bob Evans Colonial Dressing is sweet and tangy, with a strong onion and celery flavor. It is similar to a poppy seed dressing but with an added savory flavor. To help give this dressing body and stability, a little mustard and mayonnaise are added, but you can leave them out if you prefer.

YIELDS 1 CUP, 2 TABLESPOONS PER SERVING

½ cup vegetable oil
¼ cup granulated sugar
¼ cup white vinegar
2 teaspoons mayonnaise
½ teaspoon onion powder
½ teaspoon celery seed
½ teaspoon Dijon mustard

Whisk all ingredients together in a medium bowl. Use immediately or transfer to an airtight container and store up to 7 days in the refrigerator.

BOB EVANS WILDFIRE RANCH DRESSING

Typically Served With: Bob Evans Wildfire Chicken Salad

Wildfire Sauce at Bob Evans is a popular sweet and savory barbecue sauce condiment you can add as a dressing for salads or order on the side for dipping. For the Bob Evans Wildfire Chicken Salad, that sauce is mixed with equal parts ranch dressing to make a sweet and savory ranch. It is perfect for Southwest and Tex-Mex-inspired salads, but it is also wonderful spread on grilled chicken sandwiches, used as a dip for chicken nuggets, or drizzled over crispy French fries. To get the most authentic flavor, use a mild and sweet Memphis-style barbecue sauce.

YIELDS 1 CUP, 2 TABLESPOONS PER SERVING

1/2 cup sweet barbecue sauce
1/4 cup mayonnaise
1/4 cup low-fat buttermilk
1/2 teaspoon onion powder
1/4 teaspoon dried dill
1/4 teaspoon ground black pepper
1/4 teaspoon garlic powder
1/4 teaspoon sea salt

Whisk all ingredients together in a medium bowl. Transfer to an airtight container and refrigerate 4 hours before serving. Store up to 5 days in the refrigerator.

Award-Winning Sauce!

Wildfire Sauce has a winning pedigree that you may not know about. In the 1990s, the Wildfire Gourmet Cooking Team led by Paul Hood won the Memphis in May World BBQ Championship with their original Wildfire Sauce. Bob Evans became the team's sponsor and received the exclusive rights to serve a less spicy version in their restaurants.

THE CAPITAL GRILLE BLEU CHEESE DRESSING

Typically Served With: Wedge with Bleu Cheese and Smoked Bacon

The Capital Grille opened its first location in Providence, Rhode Island, in 1990. Founder Ned Grace opened his fine-dining steakhouse in a less affluent area with the idea that the high-end restaurant would attract customers, and he was right! Within 7 years, the original steakhouse was so popular, it had earned $4 million in sales. Along with delicious steaks and sides, The Capitol Grille is known for its Wedge with Bleu Cheese and Smoked Bacon. The dressing is popular because it is rich, creamy, and loaded with plenty of blue cheese.

YIELDS 1 CUP, 2 TABLESPOONS PER SERVING

1/2 cup mayonnaise
1/3 cup sour cream
1 tablespoon low-fat buttermilk
2 teaspoons white wine vinegar
1/4 teaspoon granulated sugar
1/8 teaspoon Worcestershire sauce
1/8 teaspoon cayenne pepper
1/2 cup crumbled blue cheese

In a medium bowl, whisk together mayonnaise, sour cream, buttermilk, vinegar, sugar, Worcestershire sauce, and cayenne pepper until well combined. Fold in blue cheese. Use immediately or transfer to an airtight container and refrigerate. Store up to 3 days in the refrigerator. Stir well before use.

Reducing Calories

Here are some easy swaps for reducing calories in dressings and sauces without sacrificing flavor. First, swap full-fat mayonnaise and sour cream for light or low-fat, or replace them both with fat-free Greek yogurt. Second, swap granulated sugar for low-calorie sweetener. Finally, you can reduce the oil with water or citrus juice.

THE CHEESECAKE FACTORY BALSAMIC VINAIGRETTE

Typically Served With: Factory Chopped Salad

When you get so many requests to sell your dressings that you offer them for purchase in restaurants by the pint, you know you are doing something right! The Cheesecake Factory certainly knows what they're doing when it comes to their dressings! This restaurant is loved by fans for the large, eclectic menu; delicious cheesecakes; and crave-worthy salads. Their house dressing, like all their dressings, is made from scratch each day, ensuring that guests enjoy the freshest and most vibrant flavors. Be sure to use the best-quality extra-virgin olive oil and balsamic vinegar here since their flavors really shine!

YIELDS 1 CUP, 2 TABLESPOONS PER SERVING

3/4 cup extra-virgin olive oil
3 tablespoons balsamic vinegar
3 tablespoons packed light brown sugar
1 tablespoon Dijon mustard
1 tablespoon finely minced shallot
1 clove garlic, peeled and finely minced
1/2 teaspoon sea salt
1/4 teaspoon ground black pepper

Combine all ingredients in a food processor and process until smooth, about 30 seconds. Transfer to an airtight container and refrigerate 4 hours before serving. Store up to 5 days in the refrigerator. Shake well before serving.

Balsamic Vinegar

When you are buying balsamic vinegar, check the label carefully. You want the first ingredient to be "cooked grape must," which is grape juice cooked down until thick and then aged in barrels into balsamic vinegar. Any other first ingredient means the balsamic vinegar is watered down with cheaper vinegar.

CHICK-FIL-A AVOCADO LIME RANCH DRESSING

Typically Served With: Cobb Salad

Fans of Avocado Lime Ranch Dressing enjoy sharing their love of the dressing online. Some order it with every salad on the menu. Others like to use it as a dip for Chick-fil-A's iconic Waffle Potato Fries, while still others like to add it to their favorite sandwiches, such as the Spicy Chicken Sandwich. No matter how you like to use it, this dressing is a bestseller and often cited as the best dressing on Chick-fil-A salad dressing rankings online!

YIELDS 1 CUP, 2 TABLESPOONS PER SERVING

1 large ripe avocado
1/3 cup mayonnaise
1/4 cup low-fat buttermilk
2 tablespoons fresh lime juice
1 teaspoon granulated sugar
1/2 teaspoon onion powder
1/2 teaspoon ground cumin
1/4 teaspoon dried dill
1/4 teaspoon dried chives
1/4 teaspoon ground black pepper
1/4 teaspoon garlic powder
1/4 teaspoon sea salt

1. Slice avocado in half, remove pit, and scoop flesh into a blender. Add remaining ingredients and purée 20 seconds, scrape down sides of blender, then purée again 20–30 seconds until dressing is smooth.
2. Transfer to an airtight container and refrigerate 4 hours before serving. Store up to 4 days in the refrigerator.

CHICK-FIL-A ZESTY APPLE CIDER VINAIGRETTE

Typically Served With: Grilled Market Salad

Chick-fil-A is not afraid to update and innovate when it comes to their menu, and these changes often lead to some of the most popular menu items among fans. So, when Chick-fil-A decided to add more health-conscious items to their menu in 2013, they added the Grilled Market Salad with Zesty Apple Cider Vinaigrette, and it quickly became a big success. The dressing rapidly became the most popular vinaigrette the chain has ever offered because of the tangy citrus flavor that complements grilled chicken and crisp greens. You can also use this as a dressing for a fresh fruit salad.

YIELDS 1 CUP, 2 TABLESPOONS PER SERVING

1/2 cup vegetable oil
1/4 cup apple cider vinegar
3 tablespoons honey
2 tablespoons pineapple juice
1 tablespoon fresh lemon juice
1 tablespoon granulated sugar
2 teaspoons fresh lime juice
1/2 teaspoon sea salt
1/2 teaspoon ground black pepper
1/2 teaspoon onion powder
1/4 teaspoon garlic powder

Whisk all ingredients together in a medium bowl until well mixed. Use immediately.

CHILI'S FAJITA MARINADE

Typically Used For: Steak Fajitas

Since 1984, Chili's has been grilling up their classic sizzling fajitas to happy customers. While they did not "practically invent" fajitas, despite their claims otherwise, they can be credited with helping popularize sizzling fajitas across the country. Chili's fajitas are marinated in a wet seasoning brine, and for the best flavor you should let your steak or chicken soak in the flavorful liquid at least 4 hours, but overnight is best. Reserve ¼ cup of the marinade before adding the meat to brush over the meat while grilling to keep the meat juicy.

YIELDS ¾ CUP, ENOUGH TO MARINATE 2 POUNDS OF SKIRT STEAK OR CHICKEN BREAST

¼ cup vegetable oil
¼ cup fresh lime juice
3 cloves garlic, peeled and chopped
2 tablespoons packed light brown sugar
1 teaspoon ground cumin
1 teaspoon ground black pepper
½ teaspoon sea salt
½ teaspoon paprika
½ teaspoon chili powder
¼ teaspoon dried oregano
¼ teaspoon liquid smoke

Whisk all ingredients together in a medium bowl until well mixed. Use immediately or transfer to an airtight container and refrigerate until ready to use. Store up to 7 days in the refrigerator.

History of Fajitas

Mexican ranch workers in the 1930s are thought to have invented the modern-day fajita. While working along the Texas border, they would cook unwanted cuts of beef like skirt steak over open flames and wrap them in tortillas. By 1969, the "Fajita King," Juan Antonio "Sonny" Falcón, had opened his fajita stand south of Austin, and the popularity has only grown!

CHILI'S MARGARITA GRILLED CHICKEN MARINADE

Typically Used For: Margarita Grilled Chicken

Chili's is well-known for their viral Fried Mozzarella (Chapter 10) and their delicious Fresh Salsa (Chapter 2), but they are also famous for their margaritas! Those same flavors are featured in one of the chain's most popular Guiltless Grill meals: Margarita Grilled Chicken. Here, lime and garlic are used to flavor a grilled chicken breast. In the restaurant, this is served on a bed of seasoned black beans and topped with fresh pico de gallo and crisp tortilla strips. You can also use the marinade on shrimp; just let the shrimp soak for no more than 10 minutes before grilling.

YIELDS 1 CUP, ENOUGH TO MARINATE 2 POUNDS OF CHICKEN BREAST

1 cup margarita mix, such as Tres Agaves Organic Lime Margarita Mix
1 teaspoon onion powder
1 teaspoon garlic powder
1 teaspoon ground black pepper

Whisk all ingredients together in a medium bowl until well mixed. Use immediately or transfer to an airtight container and refrigerate until ready to use. Store up to 7 days in the refrigerator.

Homemade Margarita Mix

Margarita mix is easy to make at home with a few simple ingredients. In a 2-quart pot, combine 1 cup water and ¾ cup granulated sugar. Heat over medium heat until sugar is fully melted, about 5 minutes. Cool, then stir in 1 cup fresh lime juice. Transfer to a glass bottle and chill until ready to use.

DICKEY'S BARBECUE PIT COLESLAW DRESSING

Typically Served With: Cabbage Slaw

Dickey's Barbecue Pit was founded in Dallas, Texas, by Travis Dickey in 1941 and is still family owned today. They operate over 450 locations and are known for serving slow-smoked meats, Polish sausage, and a variety of sides. One of the most popular sides is their Cabbage Slaw, which is dressed with a sweet, rich, and tangy dressing. It is delicious with smoked meats and sausage, but you can also add a scoop to your favorite chopped brisket or pulled pork sandwiches. For the full restaurant experience, you will want to chop your coleslaw mix so it resembles confetti.

YIELDS 3/4 CUP, ENOUGH TO DRESS 14 OUNCES OF COLESLAW MIX

1/2 cup mayonnaise
3 tablespoons granulated sugar
3 tablespoons apple cider vinegar
2 tablespoons lemon juice
1/2 teaspoon sea salt
1/4 teaspoon ground black pepper

Whisk together all ingredients in a medium bowl until well combined. Use immediately or transfer to an airtight container and refrigerate until ready to use. Store up to 5 days in the refrigerator.

EL POLLO LOCO CHICKEN MARINADE

Typically Used For: Fire-Grilled Chicken

When you think of El Pollo Loco, you probably think of tender grilled chicken, refreshing salsa, and soft chicken-stuffed tacos. What you may not know is that El Pollo Loco takes their commitment to freshness very seriously. They fire grill fresh, not frozen, chicken throughout the day, taking 55 minutes to cook a single bird. They also prepare their fresh salsas daily in-house and cut all their vegetables daily. This marinade is enough for a 3-pound chicken.

YIELDS 1½ CUPS, ENOUGH TO MARINATE 3 POUNDS OF BONE-IN CHICKEN PIECES

½ cup fresh pineapple juice
¼ cup fresh lime juice
¼ cup olive oil
2 tablespoons white vinegar
4 cloves garlic, peeled and minced
1 medium white onion, peeled and sliced
1 teaspoon ground cumin
1 teaspoon sea salt
1 teaspoon ground black pepper
½ teaspoon dried oregano

In a medium bowl, whisk together all ingredients until well combined. Use immediately or transfer to an airtight container and refrigerate until ready to use. Store up to 3 days in the refrigerator.

Spatchcock Chicken

To grill a whole chicken easily you can spatchcock, or butterfly, it. Flip your bird breast side down and, using culinary shears, cut out the backbone. Save that for making stock. Flip the bird back over and firmly press down with both hands until the chicken lies flat.

OLIVE GARDEN ITALIAN DRESSING

Typically Served With: House Salad

Olive Garden fans will almost always tell you that they love the salad. It is so popular that it is offered ahead of most meals, and it can also be the main meal if you order the Soup AND Salad AND Breadsticks—speaking of, you should check out the Olive Garden Breadsticks recipe in Chapter 10. The dressing is a vinaigrette with Parmesan cheese added for a salty, creamy flavor. There is also a little mayonnaise added to help keep the dressing creamy and emulsified. This dressing tastes great the same day, but if you have time to make it a day ahead, you will be glad you did!

YIELDS 1 CUP, 2 TABLESPOONS PER SERVING

1/4 cup mayonnaise
1/4 cup olive oil
1/4 cup grated Parmesan cheese
2 tablespoons white wine vinegar
2 tablespoons granulated sugar
1 tablespoon lemon juice
1/2 teaspoon Italian seasoning
1/4 teaspoon garlic powder
1/4 teaspoon sea salt

In a medium bowl, whisk together all ingredients until well combined. Transfer to an airtight container and refrigerate 4 hours before serving. Store up to 5 days in the refrigerator. Shake well before use.

Olive Garden Salad

A staple of the Olive Garden menu from day one, the House Salad is one of a few menu items made fresh daily in the restaurant along with their soups and breadsticks. The salad was so important to Olive Garden that it was included in their original slogan, "Good Times, Great Salad, Olive Garden."

OLIVE GARDEN ITALIAN DRESSING

ON THE BORDER MEXICAN GRILL & CANTINA SMOKED JALAPEÑO VINAIGRETTE

Typically Served With: Fajita Salad

When three Dallas, Texas, friends decided in 1982 that they wanted to open their own Tex-Mex restaurant, they opened On The Border South Texas Café. This restaurant eventually changed its name to On The Border Mexican Grill & Cantina and now operates over sixty locations serving Tex-Mex classics in a festive environment. This salad dressing definitely has Tex-Mex flavors, and it makes anything you add it to festive! It would be delicious on a salad, but also consider it as a marinade for chicken or shrimp or as a dip for grilled meats and vegetables.

YIELDS 1 CUP, 2 TABLESPOONS PER SERVING

1/4 cup red wine vinegar
2 tablespoons fresh lime juice
1 tablespoon granulated sugar
1 tablespoon chipotle in adobo, mashed into a paste
1/4 teaspoon ground cumin
1/4 teaspoon sea salt
1/4 teaspoon ground black pepper
1/2 cup vegetable oil

1. In a 1-quart saucepan over medium heat, add all ingredients except oil. Whisk well, then bring to a boil, reduce heat to low, and simmer 5 minutes or until dressing has thickened slightly.
2. Remove from heat and let cool to room temperature. Whisk in oil a few drops at a time until dressing is combined. Transfer to an airtight container and refrigerate 4 hours before serving. Store up to 7 days in the refrigerator. Shake well before use.

OUTBACK STEAKHOUSE TANGY TOMATO DRESSING

Typically Served With: House Side Salad

Fans of Outback Steakhouse are buzzing online about their favorite menu items, and one of them is Tangy Tomato Dressing. It has fans online searching for the recipe and chatting about how much they love it. One thread on Reddit had one user claiming they had purchased a 64-ounce container of the dressing because they loved it so much! While buying a large container of the dressing is an option, with this recipe you can make a batch anytime you like. This dressing is cooked on the stove to help the ingredients emulsify and to blend the flavors.

YIELDS 1 CUP, 2 TABLESPOONS PER SERVING

1/2 cup ketchup
1/3 cup water
1/4 cup white vinegar
1/4 cup granulated sugar
3 tablespoons olive oil
1 teaspoon tomato paste
1/2 teaspoon paprika
1/4 teaspoon garlic power
1/4 teaspoon onion powder
1/4 teaspoon ground black pepper
1/8 teaspoon cayenne pepper

1. In a 1-quart saucepan over medium heat, add all ingredients. Whisk well, then bring to a boil, reduce heat to low, and simmer 5–8 minutes until dressing has thickened slightly.
2. Remove from heat and let cool to room temperature, then transfer to an airtight container and refrigerate 4 hours before serving. Store up to 7 days in the refrigerator. Shake well before use.

Australian Inspired

Outback Steakhouse was founded in Florida in 1988 by four American partners who were inspired by Australian culture and the 1986 movie *Crocodile Dundee*. With interest in Australia surging, the founders saw an opportunity and took advantage of it. The menu has little to do with real Australian cuisine, as none of the founders even visited the nation!

PANERA BREAD ASIAN SESAME VINAIGRETTE

Typically Used With: Asian Sesame Chicken Salad

Fans of the Panera Bread Asian Sesame Chicken Salad were shocked to learn that this fan favorite salad was being removed from Panera's menu in early 2024 when they revealed their "biggest menu transformation in history." There was plenty of buzz online about missing items, but fortunately, the Asian Sesame Chicken Salad was brought back later that same year. This salad features a light, sweet, and nutty dressing with a bit of zip from the rice vinegar and pepper. No matter what Panera plans for their menu in the future, with this recipe you can enjoy the dressing on your salads anytime!

YIELDS 1 CUP, 2 TABLESPOONS PER SERVING

1/2 cup rice vinegar
1/4 cup vegetable oil
1 tablespoon sesame oil
2 tablespoons granulated sugar
1 teaspoon Dijon mustard
1/4 teaspoon ground black pepper
1/4 teaspoon onion powder
1/4 teaspoon dried parsley
1/4 teaspoon sea salt

Whisk together all ingredients until well combined. Use immediately or transfer to an airtight container and refrigerate. Store up to 5 days in the refrigerator. Shake well before use.

PANERA BREAD FUJI APPLE VINAIGRETTE

Typically Served With: Fuji Apple Chicken Salad

If there was one salad at Panera that fans adore, it has to be the Fuji Apple Chicken Salad featuring their Fuji Apple Vinaigrette. This salad dressing tastes of sweet apple, with a slight savory edge. One of the keys to the light flavor is white balsamic vinegar and apple juice, which add sweetness and tang without being too heavy. If you want to amp up the apple flavor, you can add ½ cup chopped peeled Fuji apple to a blender along with this dressing. Purée 30 seconds or until the dressing is completely smooth.

YIELDS 1 CUP, 2 TABLESPOONS PER SERVING

½ cup vegetable oil
¼ cup apple juice
3 tablespoons white balsamic vinegar
2 tablespoons honey
¼ teaspoon salt
¼ teaspoon onion powder
⅛ teaspoon garlic powder
⅛ teaspoon dried rosemary

Whisk together all ingredients until well combined. Use immediately or transfer to an airtight container and refrigerate. Store up to 5 days in the refrigerator. Shake well before use.

What Is White Balsamic Vinegar?

True balsamic vinegar is made from cooked grape must that is reduced and then aged for years in barrels until dark, sweet, and thick. White balsamic vinegar starts with grape must that is cooked until syrupy and reduced, but the similarity ends there. For white balsamic, the must is blended with white wine vinegar to produce a bright, sweet condiment.

PANERA BREAD GREEN GODDESS DRESSING

Typically Served With: Green Goddess Chicken Cobb Salad

Fans love the Green Goddess Dressing at Panera, and one of the reasons is that this dressing, unlike others, is made fresh in the restaurant. The ingredients are clean and simple, and in 2016, Dan Kish, head chef and senior vice president of food at the time, decided that if the restaurants could make a smoothie, they could make this dressing fresh in-house. This is a dressing for basil lovers! It combines fresh basil with basil pesto for layers of herby flavor. If you like, you can swap the Greek yogurt with sour cream.

YIELDS 1 CUP, 2 TABLESPOONS PER SERVING

1/2 cup loosely packed basil leaves, finely chopped
1/2 cup 1% low-fat Greek yogurt
1/4 cup mayonnaise
2 tablespoons white wine vinegar
1 tablespoon prepared basil pesto
1 tablespoon corn syrup
1 tablespoon finely minced shallot
1/2 teaspoon Dijon mustard
1/4 teaspoon sea salt
1/4 teaspoon ground black pepper

1. Add all ingredients to a food processor and pulse 10–12 times to combine and further chop basil.
2. Transfer to an airtight container and refrigerate 4 hours. Store up to 5 days in the refrigerator. Stir well before use.

The Green Goddess

Allegedly, Green Goddess dressing was created by a chef at San Francisco's Palace Hotel in 1923 in honor of the actor George Arliss, who was starring in the hit play *The Green Goddess*. Traditionally, Green Goddess dressing is made with tarragon, chives, parsley, and scallions and is a version of the French *sauce au vert* ("green sauce").

PANERA BREAD GREEN GODDESS DRESSING

P.F. CHANG'S SESAME DRESSING

Typically Served With: House Salad

Creamy, nutty, and perfect for dressing greens or used as a dip or glaze, P.F. Chang's Sesame Dressing is a modern take on Asian-style sesame dressing. One important tip: Do not use toasted sesame oil in this recipe. Toasted sesame oil has a very strong flavor that can quickly overwhelm this dressing. If you are not able to find regular sesame oil, you can replace it with an extra tablespoon of vegetable oil. Also, if you are watching your sodium, you can swap regular soy sauce for a lower-sodium version or use coconut aminos.

YIELDS 1 CUP, 2 TABLESPOONS PER SERVING

½ cup vegetable oil
2 tablespoons water
2 tablespoons soy sauce
2 tablespoons rice vinegar
2 tablespoons granulated sugar
1 tablespoon sesame oil
1 tablespoon mayonnaise
1 teaspoon toasted sesame seeds, lightly crushed

Whisk together all ingredients until well combined. Transfer to an airtight container and refrigerate 4 hours before serving. Store up to 5 days in the refrigerator. Shake well before use.

RED ROBIN SALSA-RANCH DRESSING

Typically Used With: Southwest Salad

Yes, Salsa-Ranch Dressing is a salad dressing, but it is so much more! It is also a drizzle for grilled chicken, such as in Red Robin's Ensenada Chicken Platter; it can be used to dunk their famous thick-cut Steak Fries; or it can even be used to dress up their Steamed Broccoli. Anywhere you use ranch, you can use this dressing. For the best texture, look for a smooth salsa or blend your favorite chunky salsa to smooth out the large pieces. Like it spicy? Swap out medium salsa for a hotter variety or add in 1 teaspoon of your favorite hot pepper sauce.

YIELDS 1 CUP, 2 TABLESPOONS PER SERVING

½ cup mayonnaise
½ cup prepared medium tomato salsa
¼ cup low-fat buttermilk
½ teaspoon onion powder
¼ teaspoon dried dill
¼ teaspoon dried chives
¼ teaspoon dried parsley
¼ teaspoon ground black pepper
¼ teaspoon garlic powder
¼ teaspoon sea salt

Whisk together all ingredients in a medium bowl until well combined. Use immediately or transfer to an airtight container and refrigerate. Store up to 5 days in the refrigerator. Stir well before use.

TEXAS ROADHOUSE STEAK MARINADE

Typically Used With: Steaks

Texas Roadhouse steaks are popular because they are tender, packed with flavor, and very juicy! Sure, you can just sprinkle some salt and pepper on your steak and toss it on the grill, but if you want that real Texas Roadhouse experience at home, start the day before and whip up this savory marinade. Add your steaks of choice to a resealable bag or container, pour over enough marinade to fully cover the steaks, and marinate for at least 2 hours, but overnight will yield the strongest flavor. This brine is on the salty side, so no need to add extra salt to your steaks before grilling.

YIELDS 3/4 CUP, ENOUGH TO MARINATE 2 POUNDS OF STEAK

1/4 cup soy sauce
1/4 cup olive oil
2 tablespoons balsamic vinegar
2 tablespoons Worcestershire sauce
2 tablespoons packed light brown sugar
1 teaspoon garlic powder
1 teaspoon ground black pepper
1 teaspoon onion powder
1 teaspoon dried thyme

Add all ingredients to a medium bowl and whisk to combine. Use immediately or transfer to an airtight container and refrigerate until ready to use. Store up to 7 days in the refrigerator.

Not So Texan

Texas Roadhouse is a popular Texas-themed steakhouse chain that features hand-cut steaks, delicious sides, and the most popular rolls and butter on the market. While the name says "Texas," and the decor and music are Texas inspired, the chain was founded in Indiana and is now based in Kentucky.

WENDY'S POMEGRANATE VINAIGRETTE

Typically Served with: Apple Pecan Salad

In 1992, Wendy's launched a line of to-go salads that eventually replaced the classic salad bar. The salads offered have evolved as customer tastes have changed. In 2010, Wendy's did a salad menu overhaul and added the highly popular Apple Pecan Salad dressed with Pomegranate Vinaigrette—the only salad from that era that remains on the menu today! The salad is the perfect blend of sweet and savory, and the dressing keeps things refreshing and tangy with orange and pomegranate flavors. When making this at home, pomegranate molasses adds the right tang and sweetness. It can be found in most grocery stores and online.

YIELDS 1 CUP, 2 TABLESPOONS PER SERVING

¼ cup vegetable oil
¼ cup orange juice
¼ cup pomegranate molasses
1 tablespoon white wine vinegar
1 tablespoon balsamic vinegar
1 tablespoon Dijon mustard
1 teaspoon fresh orange zest
¼ teaspoon ground black pepper
¼ teaspoon garlic powder
¼ teaspoon onion powder

Whisk together all ingredients in a medium bowl until well combined. Use immediately or transfer to an airtight container and refrigerate. Store up to 5 days in the refrigerator. Shake well before use.

Pomegranate Molasses

Add 2 cups pomegranate juice and ¼ cup granulated sugar to a 2-quart saucepan. Heat over high heat, stirring constantly, and bring to a boil. Reduce heat to medium-low and simmer, stirring often, until mixture is reduced enough to coat the back of a spoon, 30–40 minutes. Cool and store in an airtight container in the refrigerator up to 6 months.

CHAPTER 7

ON THE SIDE: SIDE DISH DIPPING SAUCES

Side dishes are better when you have a dip to enjoy them with! A plate of pretzel bites is great, but when you pair those pretzel bites with a cheesy dip, they become irresistible. French fries are great on their own, and better with ketchup, but a creamy fry sauce with a tangy zip takes them to a new level. Even lettuce wraps, which are always a popular appetizer or light meal, are better with a bit of dipping sauce to make the flavors pop. This chapter has recipes for all the best side dish dipping sauces so you can have any sauce you like for any meal or occasion. Make your French fries, Tater Tots, and steak fries the star of the show with some Shake Shack Cheese Sauce or Freddy's Frozen Custard & Steakburgers Famous Fry Sauce. Pretzel bites on the menu? Make a batch of Culver's Wisconsin Cheddar Cheese Sauce and watch them disappear. Chicken nuggets get a bit of nostalgic zip from McDonald's Szechuan Sauce, and if fried onion petals are what you crave, you should make a batch of Outback Steakhouse Bloomin' Onion Sauce. When it comes to stepping up your side dish sauce game, you can't go wrong with these recipes!

APPLEBEE'S NEIGHBORHOOD GRILL + BAR BEER CHEESE DIP

Typically Served With: Brew Pub Pretzels

Pretzels and beer cheese dip are a popular snack and appetizer, and Applebee's has taken the cheese dip to the next level by using Blue Moon Belgian White Belgian-Style Wheat Ale. This specific beer gives the dip a bright, tangy flavor with a hit of citrus and is important for achieving the right flavor in the finished dip. A bit of Dijon mustard and a touch of hot sauce add depth to the flavors. While white Cheddar is called for here, you can swap in any Cheddar you have on hand without impacting the flavor.

SERVES 8

1/4 cup unsalted butter
1/4 cup all-purpose flour
1 clove garlic, peeled and minced
1 (12-ounce) bottle Blue Moon Belgian White Belgian-Style Wheat Ale
1 tablespoon Dijon mustard
1/4 teaspoon Worcestershire sauce
2 cups shredded white Cheddar cheese
1 cup shredded Colby jack cheese
1 teaspoon hot pepper sauce
1/4 teaspoon onion powder

1. In a 2-quart pot over medium heat, add butter. Once butter is melted and foaming, add flour and garlic and whisk with a silicone whisk to combine. Cook, whisking constantly, 3 minutes or until the flour turns lightly golden brown. Reduce heat to low and slowly whisk in beer until smooth. Whisk in Dijon mustard and Worcestershire sauce.
2. Once mixture is smooth, reduce heat to low and whisk in cheese in three increments, making sure the cheese is fully melted before adding more. Once mixture is again smooth, add hot pepper sauce and onion powder and whisk well. Serve immediately.

ARBY'S BRONCO BERRY SAUCE

Typically Served With: Jalapeño Bites

Despite having "berry" in the name, you will not find any berries on the ingredient list for Bronco Berry Sauce. Instead, the sauce is made with a mild pepper jelly base with a hint of heat from jalapeño. This recipe uses red pepper jelly and jalapeño pepper jelly to replicate that flavor. These are available in most grocery stores, but you can easily get them online if you can't find them on the shelves. If you like it extra spicy, you can swap all or some of the red pepper jelly for hot red pepper jelly. To add a vibrant red color, add 2 or 3 drops of red food coloring after cooling.

YIELDS 1 CUP, 2 TABLESPOONS PER SERVING

¾ cup red pepper jelly
3 tablespoons jalapeño pepper jelly
1 tablespoon Thai sweet chili sauce
1 tablespoon water

In a 1-quart saucepan over low heat, add all ingredients and mix well. Heat until both jellies are melted and the mixture is well combined. Remove from heat and cool to room temperature before serving or transfer to an airtight container and refrigerate up to 7 days.

What about the Berries?

You may be wondering why Bronco Berry Sauce has a berry flavor without actually containing any berries. There are a couple of factors at play. First, the bright red color suggests berries. Second, the mix of sugar and vinegar flavors simulates the tart-sweet flavor of berries. All this fools your taste buds and brain into tasting berries!

CARRABBA'S ITALIAN GRILL DIPPING OIL

Typically Served With: Warm Bread

At Carrabba's, when your server greets you, they deliver a basket of warm bread and a plate with garlic and herbs that is transformed with a few swirls of extra-virgin olive oil into a savory dip. This herb and oil dip is perfect for dunking chunks of bread, and it's a delicious way to start a meal. The herbs for this mix should not be prepared more than 4 hours in advance to preserve their color and fresh flavor. Aside from bread, you can use the garlic-herb mixture as a seasoning for baked chicken or fish.

SERVES 4

1 tablespoon finely chopped fresh basil leaves
1 tablespoon finely chopped fresh Italian parsley
1 tablespoon finely minced garlic
1 teaspoon dried thyme
1 teaspoon dried oregano
1 teaspoon sea salt
1 teaspoon ground black pepper
1/2 teaspoon finely chopped fresh rosemary
1/4 teaspoon crushed red pepper flakes
1/4 teaspoon fresh lemon juice
1/2 cup extra-virgin olive oil

1. In a food processor, add all ingredients except lemon juice and oil. Pulse until mixture is very finely chopped. Transfer to a plate and stir in lemon juice and oil. Serve immediately with warm bread for dipping.
2. If not using immediately, transfer herb mixture from food processor to an airtight container and refrigerate 4 hours. Use herb mixture the same day it is prepared.

A Matter of Hospitality

Have you ever wondered why most Italian restaurants serve free bread before the meal? It's a way to show guests that they are welcome and appreciated. In Italian culture, bread is commonly served with most meals, so offering it is an important food custom and reflects Italian hospitality.

CARRABBA'S ITALIAN GRILL DIPPING OIL

THE CHEESECAKE FACTORY SOY-GINGER SESAME SAUCE

Typically Served With: Chicken Pot Stickers

The Cheesecake Factory is a great place to dine with family and friends because they offer a wide array of dishes from various cuisines. For lovers of Asian cuisine, Chicken Pot Stickers are a popular appetizer choice. They are served with a savory sauce that sports garlic, ginger, and a delicious mix of toasted sesame and tangy rice vinegar. You can enjoy this sauce with dumplings or pot stickers or as a dip for grilled chicken and shrimp. It is also great as an accompaniment to fried panko-crusted shrimp or chicken or as a drizzle for a poke bowl!

YIELDS 1 CUP, 2 TABLESPOONS PER SERVING

1/2 cup soy sauce
1/4 cup rice vinegar
2 tablespoons granulated sugar
2 teaspoons sesame oil
1 clove garlic, peeled and minced
1 teaspoon minced fresh ginger
1 tablespoon thinly sliced green onion, green parts only
1/2 teaspoon minced fresh cilantro
1/4 teaspoon toasted sesame seeds

1. In a 1-quart saucepan over medium heat, combine soy sauce, vinegar, sugar, oil, garlic, and ginger. Heat, mixing often, until sugar is melted, about 3 minutes. Remove from stove and cool to room temperature.
2. To serve, transfer sauce to a dipping bowl. Top with green onions, cilantro, and sesame seeds. Serve immediately.
3. Transfer leftover sauce to an airtight container and refrigerate up to 3 days.

THE CHEESECAKE FACTORY TAMARIND-CASHEW DIPPING SAUCE

Typically Served With: Avocado Eggrolls

Tamarind has a distinctly sweet and sour flavor and is the key to what makes this dip so tangy and delicious! It can be a little tricky to find, but most well-stocked Asian markets have it on hand; otherwise, you can purchase it online. This dip is usually served with Avocado Eggrolls, but it is also wonderful as a dip for fried or baked wonton chips or drizzled over freshly grilled chicken or fish. You can make this sauce a day or two ahead, but it is best when enjoyed within a few days of making.

YIELDS 1 CUP, 2 TABLESPOONS PER SERVING

1/3 cup honey
1 tablespoon granulated sugar
1 tablespoon balsamic vinegar
1/2 teaspoon tamarind pulp
1/2 cup chopped roasted, unsalted cashews
1/2 cup lightly packed fresh cilantro leaves
2 green onions, roughly chopped
2 cloves garlic, peeled
1/2 teaspoon ground cumin
1/4 teaspoon ground black pepper
1/4 cup olive oil

1. In a microwave-safe bowl, combine honey, sugar, vinegar, and tamarind. Heat 30 seconds, then stir until sugar and tamarind are melted.
2. Add honey mixture and all ingredients except oil to blender. Purée 30 seconds, then slowly drizzle in oil until fully incorporated. Serve immediately or transfer to an airtight container and refrigerate until ready to use. Store leftover sauce up to 3 days in the refrigerator.

Tamarind

Tamarind comes from a tree that produces brown pods with a tart-sweet pulp. It is a popular ingredient in Southeast Asian, Caribbean, and Indian cuisines. Tamarind paste is one of the primary flavors in pad thai, and it is delicious added to Indian curries, chutneys, and cocktails.

THE CHEESECAKE FACTORY THAI PEANUT SAUCE

Typically Served With: Thai Lettuce Wraps with Chicken

This luxurious sauce is creamy and rich and has a pleasantly sweet and nutty flavor. It is perfect to drizzle over grilled chicken or avocado nestled in crisp lettuce cups. This sauce also makes a tasty dressing for a grilled chicken salad, shredded cabbage slaw, or even freshly cooked rice noodles. Like many of The Cheesecake Factory's signature sauces, it is available to purchase in larger-format containers, which is something fans often take advantage of. With this recipe, you don't need to make a trip to the restaurant and can whip up a batch at home anytime a craving strikes!

YIELDS ½ CUP, 2 TABLESPOONS PER SERVING

¼ cup creamy peanut butter
¼ cup granulated sugar
2 tablespoons fresh lime juice
1 tablespoon soy sauce
2 teaspoons rice vinegar
1 teaspoon water
½ teaspoon sriracha

1. In a 1-quart saucepan over medium heat, combine all ingredients. Heat, mixing often, until peanut butter is melted, about 3 minutes.
2. Remove from stove and cool to room temperature before serving. Transfer leftover sauce to an airtight container and store up to 7 days. Bring to room temperature before serving.

Allergy-Friendly Swaps

Those with peanut allergies can swap smooth almond or sunflower butter for the peanut butter, and those who are gluten-free can swap coconut aminos for the soy sauce. Be sure to check your sriracha label, and if it contains allergens, you can swap it for your favorite allergy-free hot sauce.

THE CHEESECAKE FACTORY THAI PEANUT SAUCE

CULVER'S WISCONSIN CHEDDAR CHEESE SAUCE

Typically Served With: Pretzel Bites

Culver's prides themselves on fresh ingredients and delicious food. Among the most popular items on the menu is their Wisconsin Cheddar Cheese Sauce. It is made primarily of aged Wisconsin Cheddar cheese and other dairy, and fans dip everything from pretzels and French fries to chicken and even burgers in it! Aged Cheddar is going to give you the best, most tangy flavor. For the best texture, grate the cheese fresh. Pre-grated cheese is coated in anti-caking agents that can make the sauce grainy.

SERVES 6

2 tablespoons unsalted butter
2 tablespoons all-purpose flour
1 cup whole milk
2 cups freshly grated aged sharp Cheddar cheese
1/2 teaspoon sea salt

1. In a 2-quart saucepan over medium heat add butter. Once butter is melted and foaming, add flour and whisk to combine. Cook, whisking constantly, until flour is cooked through, about 2 minutes.
2. Reduce heat to low and slowly whisk in milk, making sure no lumps of flour remain. Increase heat to medium and cook, whisking constantly, 2 minutes.
3. Reduce heat to low and add cheese and salt. Whisk until cheese is melted and sauce is smooth. Serve immediately.
4. Transfer leftover sauce to an airtight container and refrigerate up to 3 days. Reheat leftover sauce in a saucepan over low heat until melted and hot.

DOMINO'S CHEESY MARINARA DIP

Typically Served With: Handmade Bread Twists

Oven-baked dips have become some of the most popular items at Domino's, and people are sharing their love for these dips all over social media! This version has a tangy marinara sauce base, a layer of prepared Alfredo sauce for extra creaminess, and lots of shredded mozzarella. Whole milk mozzarella will have the best stretchy texture, which is part of what makes this dip fun to eat—who does not love a cheese pull? This dip is meant to be enjoyed with garlic bread, so a great accompaniment to it would be a batch of Olive Garden Breadsticks (Chapter 10).

SERVES 6

2 cups chunky marinara sauce
½ cup Alfredo sauce
1 cup shredded whole milk mozzarella cheese

1. Preheat oven to 400°F and spray an 8" × 8" square pan with nonstick cooking spray.
2. In prepared dish, add marinara sauce and spread evenly. Drizzle Alfredo sauce over top as evenly as possible, then spread cheese evenly over top.
3. Bake 20–25 minutes until edges are bubbling and cheese is melted and starting to brown. Cool 3 minutes before serving.

Oven-Baked Goodness

Domino's introduced oven-baked dips in 2021 with their Cheesy Marinara, Five Cheese, and Baked Apple Dips. Along with the dips were bread twists—Parmesan or Garlic Bread Twists for the savory dips, Cinnamon Bread Twists for the Baked Apple. Today, the Baked Apple Dip is no more, but the two savory dips and Cinnamon Bread Twists are still available.

FREDDY'S FROZEN CUSTARD & STEAKBURGERS FAMOUS FRY SAUCE

Typically Served With: Freddy's Fries

Freddy's is famous for smashburgers, Vienna beef hot dogs, and crisp, golden brown shoestring fries served with their Famous Fry Sauce. This sauce is a creamy blend of mayonnaise, spices, ketchup, and a splash of dill pickle brine. While it may be sold as a fry sauce, it is truly an everything sauce! It is excellent for fries, burgers, chicken tenders, onion rings, Tater Tots, and almost anything you can imagine. Fans of Freddy's, dubbed FredHeads, love to share their favorite menu items on social media.

YIELDS 1 CUP, 2 TABLESPOONS PER SERVING

3/4 cup mayonnaise
1/4 cup ketchup
1 teaspoon dill pickle brine
1 teaspoon yellow mustard
1/2 teaspoon paprika
1/4 teaspoon onion powder
1/4 teaspoon Worcestershire sauce
1/8 teaspoon ground black pepper

In a medium bowl, whisk together all ingredients until well combined. Use immediately or transfer to an airtight container and refrigerate. Store up to 5 days in the refrigerator. Sitr well before use.

Social Media Love

When it comes to social media, Freddy's is at the top of their game! They post the standard photos and news, but they also like to post games, polls, and memes to entertain fans. Their social media team also frequently reposts fan photos and reels, making sure they give full credit, to share the love.

MCDONALD'S SZECHUAN SAUCE

Typically Served With: Chicken McNuggets

In 1998, the movie ***Mulan*** was released, and as a promotional tie-in, McDonald's introduced a Chinese-style dipping sauce called Szechuan Sauce as part of a Chicken McNuggets Happy Meal. After the promotion period ended, the sauce was retired. However, its story took a turn thanks to the show ***Rick and Morty***. In a 2017 episode, the character Rick rants about wanting Szechuan Sauce, which sparked renewed interest in the long-retired condiment. The demand was so high that McDonald's decided to re-release the sauce in 2017 and again in 2018 and 2022 for a limited time. Although it may be unavailable again, you can still enjoy the viral sauce anytime you like with this recipe!

YIELDS 1 CUP, 2 TABLESPOONS PER SERVING

1½ cups water, divided
½ cup soy sauce
1-inch piece fresh ginger, peeled and sliced
4 cloves garlic, peeled and smashed
¼ cup packed light brown sugar
½ teaspoon toasted sesame oil
¼ teaspoon Szechuan peppercorn powder
¼ teaspoon ground coriander
2 tablespoons cornstarch
1 tablespoon rice vinegar
2 tablespoons fresh lime juice

1. In a 2-quart saucepan, combine 1 cup water, soy sauce, ginger, and garlic. Heat over medium heat until mixture comes to a boil. Reduce heat to low and simmer 10 minutes, then cover pot and remove from heat. Let stand at room temperature 20 minutes.
2. Strain liquid into a bowl and discard solids. Return liquid to pot and add brown sugar, sesame oil, Szechuan peppercorn powder, and coriander. Heat over medium heat until mixture comes to a boil.
3. In a small bowl, whisk together remaining water with cornstarch and then whisk mixture into pot. Reduce heat to medium-low and cook, whisking constantly, 1 minute. Remove from heat and stir in vinegar and lime juice. Cool to room temperature before serving.
4. Transfer leftover sauce to an airtight container and store up to 7 days in the refrigerator.

Making Szechuan Peppercorn Powder at Home

Place 2 tablespoons Szechuan peppercorns in a dry skillet over medium heat. Toast peppercorns 3–5 minutes until they start to pop and are fragrant. Cool peppercorns, then grind in a spice grinder or mortar and pestle. Sift through a strainer and discard large husks. Enjoy!

MIMI'S CAFE CREAMY MORNAY CHEESE SAUCE

Typically Served With: Breakfast Crepes

Airman Arthur Simms was stationed in France during World War II, where, during a party held to celebrate the country's liberation, he met a woman named Mimi. This woman inspired the name he would eventually call his restaurant—Mimi's Cafe. Known for casual French food, Mimi's offers breakfast, lunch, and dinner. One of the most popular breakfast dishes is the Breakfast Crepes, which are smothered in creamy, cheesy Mornay sauce. This classic French sauce is seasoned with a dash of nutmeg and a blend of Gruyère and Parmesan cheeses.

SERVES 6

2 tablespoons unsalted butter
2 tablespoons all-purpose flour
1½ cups whole milk
¼ large white onion, peeled
1 bay leaf
1 whole clove
½ cup grated Gruyère cheese
2 tablespoons grated Parmesan cheese
¼ teaspoon sea salt
⅛ teaspoon ground nutmeg
⅛ teaspoon hot pepper sauce, such as Tabasco

1. In a 2-quart saucepan over medium heat, add butter. Once butter is melted and foaming, sprinkle in flour and cook, stirring constantly, until flour is starting to just turn lightly golden, about 3 minutes. Reduce heat to low and whisk in milk until smooth, then add onion, bay leaf, and clove.
2. Continue to cook, stirring constantly, until sauce starts to simmer, about 5 minutes. Remove sauce from heat and stir in Gruyère, Parmesan, salt, nutmeg, and hot sauce. When sauce is smooth, remove bay leaf, onion, and clove. Serve immediately.

French Sauces

The French are well-known for their delicious food. Sauces are a staple of French cuisine, and aspiring chefs learn to make them as part of their training. The five French mother sauces, as they are called, are the basis for almost every popular French sauce known today. These sauces are hollandaise, béchamel, velouté, espagnole, and tomato.

OUTBACK STEAKHOUSE BLOOMIN' ONION SAUCE

Typically Served With: Bloomin' Onion

The Bloomin' Onion is one of the best known and best loved appetizers on the Outback Steakhouse menu. A whole onion is sliced, battered, and deep-fried so the individual pieces look like a blooming flower, hence the name. Served with the onion is a creamy dip, flavored with horseradish, that is strangely rich yet refreshing. While this sauce is best known as a dip for the famous Bloomin' Onion, it is also excellent used as a dip for French fries, battered seafood, or roasted vegetables or spread on toasted hamburger buns. If you have time, make this sauce a day ahead to develop the flavors.

YIELDS 3/4 CUP, 2 TABLESPOONS PER SERVING

1/2 cup mayonnaise
2 teaspoons ketchup
2 tablespoons cream-style horseradish
1/4 teaspoon paprika, divided
1/4 teaspoon salt
1/8 teaspoon dried oregano
1/8 teaspoon ground black pepper
1/8 teaspoon cayenne pepper

In a small bowl, mix together all ingredients. Cover and refrigerate until ready to serve.

Russell's Marina Grill

Jeff Glowski, one of the founders of Outback Steakhouse, was working at Russell's Marina Grill in New Orleans in 1985. The chef, Tim Gannon, came up with a battered and deep-fried onion cut to look like a blooming flower. This recipe would eventually follow Jeff to the Outback Steakhouse, where it is one of their signature recipes.

OUTBACK STEAKHOUSE BLOOMIN' ONION SAUCE

OUTBACK STEAKHOUSE CREOLE MARMALADE

Typically Served With: Gold Coast Coconut Shrimp

In Queensland, Australia, the Gold Coast is a popular vacation destination for Australians and tourists alike, loved for its diverse geography and beautiful beaches. When the owners of Outback Steakhouse were devising their Australian-themed menu, it made sense to name a seafood appetizer after one of the best-known coastal destinations in the country. Gold Coast Coconut Shrimp are lightly breaded and rolled in coconut before being fried until crisp. They are served with a sweet and tangy orange sauce that complements the sweet coconut while adding a spicy zip to keep your mouth watering!

YIELDS 1 CUP, 2 TABLESPOONS PER SERVING

3/4 cup plus 2 tablespoons orange marmalade
1 tablespoon stone ground mustard
1 tablespoon prepared horseradish
1/4 teaspoon sea salt

In a medium bowl, whisk together all ingredients until well combined. Transfer to an airtight container and refrigerate 4 hours before serving. Store up to 5 days in the refrigerator. Serve at room temperature.

What Is Marmalade?

While jam and jelly are thickened by the addition of fruit pectin, marmalade is thickened from the natural pectin found in the peel of citrus fruit. That is why most commercial marmalade has small bits of citrus peel inside. Marmalade is most often made with citrus like orange, grapefruit, lemon, or lime.

PAPA JOHNS SPECIAL GARLIC DIPPING SAUCE

Typically Served With: Pizza

Papa Johns Special Garlic Dipping Sauce was added to the menu in 1984 by founder John Schnatter and remains one of the most popular dips they offer. Fans will order extra tubs of the sauce for dipping everything from pizza and breadsticks to wings, and—in a YouTube video by Guga Foods—it was even used to deep-fry a steak! While it may not be recommended to use for frying, it can be used to make garlic bread, added to equal parts hot sauce for a wing sauce, or brushed onto pizza crust before baking to add extra buttery flavor.

YIELDS 1 CUP, 2 TABLESPOONS PER SERVING

1 cup liquid margarine, such as Parkay
1 teaspoon garlic powder
1/4 teaspoon onion powder

Whisk together all ingredients in a medium bowl until well combined. Transfer to an airtight container and refrigerate 4 hours before serving. Store up to 5 days in the refrigerator. To serve, place sauce in a microwave-safe bowl and heat on medium power 30–45 seconds until melted.

Humble Beginnings

In 1984, Papa Johns was founded in a broom closet of Mick's Lounge in Jeffersonville, Indiana. John Schnatter sold his car to purchase his pizza oven, and his pizzas were so popular, he was able to move into a larger space the next year. Today, the chain has over five thousand locations!

P.F. CHANG'S CHICKEN LETTUCE WRAP DIPPING SAUCE

Typically Served With: Chang's Chicken Lettuce Wraps

One of the most popular and most duplicated recipes from P.F. Chang's is their Chang's Chicken Lettuce Wraps. What makes these so popular is the combination of hot seasoned chicken, cool and crisp lettuce, and the tangy sweet sauce drizzled over the top of the wraps at the table. That sauce is pretty easy to make and can be used for dipping lettuce wraps, but it can also be used as a salad dressing or a marinade for grilled or baked chicken. If you prefer to skip the rice wine, you can replace it with rice vinegar.

YIELDS 1 CUP, 2 TABLESPOONS PER SERVING

1/4 cup soy sauce
1/4 cup rice cooking wine, such as michiu
1/4 cup granulated sugar
1/4 cup oyster sauce
1/4 teaspoon ground white pepper

In a 2-quart saucepan, combine all ingredients. Heat over low heat until sugar is melted, about 5 minutes. Remove from heat and cool to room temperature before transferring to an airtight container and refrigerating 4 hours before serving. Store up to 4 days in the refrigerator. Serve at room temperature.

RED ROBIN HONEY MUSTARD POPPYSEED SAUCE

Typically Served With: Clucks & Fries

Red Robin's combination of poppyseed and honey mustard dressings is a huge hit among fans! People on social media share their versions of their Honey Mustard Poppyseed Sauce or dedicate posts to their love of the condiment. The sauce is a general dipping sauce on the menu and can be used for chicken tenders, sandwiches, wraps or chicken sandwiches or as a dressing for your favorite salad. The mix of Dijon and yellow mustards is part of what makes this dressing so tasty, because blending the two adds just the right mix of tangy and spicy. If you only want to use one type, 2 tablespoons of Dijon will have the better flavor.

YIELDS 1¼ CUPS, 2 TABLESPOONS PER SERVING

¾ cup mayonnaise
2 tablespoons granulated sugar
2 tablespoons honey
1 tablespoon yellow mustard
1 tablespoon Dijon mustard
1 tablespoon vegetable oil
1 tablespoon white vinegar
1 tablespoon poppy seeds

In a medium bowl, whisk together all ingredients until well combined. Transfer to an airtight container and refrigerate 4 hours before serving. Store up to 5 days in the refrigerator.

SHAKE SHACK CHEESE SAUCE

Typically Served With: Fries

Cheese fries are a popular burger restaurant side dish usually made with fries covered in a slice of American cheese or nacho cheese sauce. The Shake Shack version takes this classic and elevates the flavors and texture. This copycat version is flavored with white wine, jalapeños, and peppercorns for an elegant, gourmet flavor. The secret to the smooth texture is deli-sliced American cheese, which keeps the sauce silky smooth. The best-quality American cheese is found in your grocery store's deli department—ask for 5 ounces to make this recipe.

YIELDS 2 CUPS, 1/4 CUP PER SERVING

1 tablespoon vegetable oil
1/4 cup sliced yellow onion
1 tablespoon thin sliced jalapeños
1 tablespoon whole peppercorns
1/8 teaspoon salt
2 teaspoons white wine vinegar
2 teaspoons dry white wine
1 cup heavy cream
1 cup cubed yellow American cheese
1 cup shredded mild Cheddar cheese

1. In a medium saucepan over medium heat, add oil. Once oil is hot, add onion, jalapeño, peppercorns, and salt. Sauté until vegetables are tender, about 5 minutes.
2. Add vinegar and wine and reduce until 1 teaspoon of liquid remains, 1–2 minutes. Stir in heavy cream, remove pan from heat, and steep 30 minutes.
3. Strain steeped cream into a small bowl. Discard solids. Return cream to pot and heat over medium-high heat until it comes to a boil, about 3 minutes. Reduce heat to medium-low and whisk in cheeses until smooth. Enjoy immediately.

SONIC GROOVY SAUCE

Typically Served With: Groovy Fries

In 2024, Sonic made some updates to their menu, which included adding a new smash-burger and making some big changes to their French fries. They replaced their old fries, smooth-cut fries that had been unchanged for 10 years, with their new Groovy Fries. These new crinkle-cut fries have a crisp coating and are perfect for dipping into their new signature Groovy Sauce. With a ranch dressing base brightened up with a bit of ketchup and sriracha, the sauce has a flavor that keeps you coming back for more! Groovy Sauce may be designed with fries in mind, but fans love it on Sonic's iconic Tots and for dunking chicken.

YIELDS 1 CUP, 2 TABLESPOONS PER SERVING

3/4 cup mayonnaise
2 tablespoons buttermilk
1 tablespoon ketchup
2 teaspoons sriracha
1/2 teaspoon onion powder
1/4 teaspoon dried dill
1/4 teaspoon dried chives
1/4 teaspoon dried parsley
1/4 teaspoon ground black pepper
1/4 teaspoon garlic powder
1/4 teaspoon sea salt

Whisk together all ingredients until well combined. Transfer to an airtight container and refrigerate 4 hours before serving. Store up to 5 days in the refrigerator.

The Top Hat

In 1953, Troy N. Smith Sr. opened a root beer stand named the Top Hat that sold burgers and hot dogs. The stand eventually added parking and speakers to order food, and the drive-in was born. In 1959, Smith learned that "Top Hat" was already trademarked, so he changed the name to Sonic.

TACO BELL NACHO CHEESE SAUCE

Typically Served With: Chips

While Taco Bell Nacho Cheese Sauce is typically served with chips, the reality is that this creamy cheese sauce is featured on so much more—from nachos and burritos to specialty items like Nacho Fries and Crunchwrap Supremes. You can also order extra Nacho Cheese Sauce on the side so you can add more or, like many viral mukbangs out there, drizzle it over your food before taking a big bite! For the best flavor you will want to get the American cheese from your grocery store's deli department. If that is unavailable, you can substitute Velveeta Original Cheese or Kraft Deli Deluxe American Cheese Slices.

YIELDS 1¼ CUP, ¼ CUP PER SERVING

8 ounces American cheese, cubed
¼ cup evaporated milk
3 tablespoons pickled jalapeño brine

In a 1-quart saucepan, combine all ingredients. Place pan over medium heat and cook, stirring constantly, until cheese is melted and sauce is smooth, about 5 minutes. Remove from heat and serve immediately.

Ballpark Nachos

In 1976, Frank Liberto, owner of Ricos Products, served a version of nachos that included warm nacho cheese sauce and prepared tortilla chips. Called ballpark nachos, this version was sold at the old Arlington Stadium in Arlington, Texas. By 1978, Liberto's version was available at the Dallas Cowboys' stadium, where *Monday Night Football* broadcaster Howard Cosell started using the word "nachos" to describe plays, and their popularity grew from there!

WENDY'S GHOST PEPPER RANCH SAUCE

Typically Served With: Saucy Nuggs

Wendy's has never been afraid of offering fans bold, spicy menu options. Fans love their Spicy Nuggs and fiery sauces like their Ghost Pepper Ranch. Ghost Pepper Ranch is so popular that Wendy's dedicated an entire limited-time menu to the spicy condiment! In 2023, they announced the addition of a Spicy Ghost Pepper Ranch Chicken Sandwich and Ghost Pepper Fries, which they said were the perfect combination for people who like to double down on spice. Sadly, that promotion ended, but in 2024 they introduced Saucy Nuggs, which includes a Spicy Ghost Pepper option for coating your chicken nuggets.

YIELDS 1 CUP, 2 TABLESPOONS PER SERVING

½ cup mayonnaise
¼ cup low-fat buttermilk
¼ cup sour cream
2 tablespoons ghost pepper hot sauce
½ teaspoon onion powder
¼ teaspoon dried dill
¼ teaspoon dried chives
¼ teaspoon dried parsley
¼ teaspoon ground black pepper
¼ teaspoon garlic powder
¼ teaspoon sea salt
¼ teaspoon ghost pepper powder

In a medium bowl, whisk together all ingredients until well combined. Use immediately or transfer to an airtight container and refrigerate. Store up to 5 days in the refrigerator. Stir well before use.

Ghost Peppers

Also known as the "bhut jolokia," the ghost pepper is native to Northeast India. It has 1,001,304 Scoville Heat Units, making it an exceptionally hot pepper. From 2007 to 2011, it was certified as the hottest pepper by *Guinness World Records* until it was replaced by the Trinidad Scorpion Butch T pepper.

WENDY'S GHOST PEPPER RANCH SAUCE

CHAPTER 8

THE FINISHING TOUCH: COOKING, FINISHING, AND TOPPING SAUCES

Fancy meals or fun finger foods are best when finished with the perfect sauce. Breakfast, lunch, or dinner, there's no meal that can't be made more special or more elegant with a drizzle or coating of a complementary sauce. This chapter will give you options for sauces to dress up pancakes, coat chicken wings, drizzle over cinnamon rolls, or smother smoked brisket. Even ice cream treats get the finishing sauce treatment with options for rich and chocolaty or sweet and fruity. Breakfast lovers will go wild for Snooze, an A.M. Eatery Smoked Cheddar Hollandaise or IHOP Butter Pecan Syrup. Love buffalo wings? Buffalo Wild Wings Asian Zing Sauce or Hooters Daytona Beach Sauce are the answer! Dinners are made more elegant with Fogo de Chão Chimichurri Sauce for a perfectly grilled steak or with Panda Express Kung Pao Sauce for coating stir-fried chicken and vegetables. For dessert, smother a mile-high bowl of ice cream in Dairy Queen Hot Fudge or Strawberry Topping—or both! With the recipes in this chapter, you can complete your meal the way you want with the perfect sauce as the finishing touch.

BENIHANA MUSTARD SAUCE

Typically Served With: Hibachi Entrées

If you are having a hibachi night at home and want a versatile dipping sauce to enjoy with vegetables, beef, chicken, or seafood, you have come to the right place! Benihana Mustard Sauce is tart, rich, and perfect for enjoying with your favorite meats and vegetables. Toasted sesame seeds give this sauce its rich flavor, so if you can't find the seeds toasted, you will want to do so yourself by cooking in a dry skillet over medium heat 2–5 minutes until fragrant. You can also enjoy this sauce drizzled over steaks or stir-fry or as a finishing sauce for fried rice or stir-fried noodles.

YIELDS 1 CUP, 2 TABLESPOONS PER SERVING

3 tablespoons heavy whipping cream
3 tablespoons dry mustard powder
2 tablespoons toasted sesame seeds
2 tablespoons hot water
3/4 cup soy sauce
1 clove garlic, peeled and roughly chopped

Add all ingredients to a blender. Purée on high 30 seconds or until mixture is smooth. Serve immediately or transfer to an airtight container and refrigerate until ready to use. Store up to 3 days in the refrigerator.

Adventurous Advertising

For 34 years, Hiroaki "Rocky" Aoki held the world record for the longest hot air balloon flight when he flew a hot air balloon emblazoned with the Benihana name from Japan to California. The flight took place in 1981 and was over 5,000 miles long! Other promotions included beauty pageants and branded race cars and powerboats.

BOB EVANS SAUSAGE GRAVY

Typically Served With: Biscuits

When you are craving comfort, nothing beats fluffy buttermilk biscuits smothered in creamy sausage gravy! Or maybe you are looking for a delicious topping for a breakfast casserole, breakfast potatoes, a savory potato and egg breakfast bowl, or even dinner dishes like pork chops or chicken tenders. Bob Evans is known for their comfort food dishes, and their Sausage Gravy is a comfort food staple. This gravy comes together in a snap and can be made ahead of time and reheated on the stove in a saucepan over low heat until hot and steamy.

SERVES 4

1 pound Bob Evans Original Roll Pork Sausage
1/4 cup all-purpose flour
2 cups whole milk
1/2 teaspoon salt
1/2 teaspoon ground black pepper

1. In a large skillet over medium heat, add sausage. Cook, crumbling well, until browned, about 8 minutes. Stir in flour and cook 1 minute. Gradually stir in milk, mixing until smooth.
2. Cook gravy until thick and bubbly, 5–7 minutes, stirring constantly. Season with salt and pepper and stir well. Serve immediately.

Owens Sausage

In 1987, Bob Evans purchased the Owens sausage brand, founded in 1928 by Clifford Owens in Texas, who sold his secret recipe sausage to friends and then expanded across Texas, Oklahoma, and Louisiana. If you can't find Bob Evans Original Roll Pork Sausage, Owens Original Pork Sausage Roll is an excellent and flavorful alternative.

BUFFALO WILD WINGS ASIAN ZING SAUCE

Typically Served With: Buffalo Wings

With over 1,300 locations across the United States, Buffalo Wild Wings is one of the most popular places to enjoy buffalo wings, cold beers, and your favorite sports on their many large-screen televisions. Buffalo Wild Wings has a large menu of wing sauces and dry rubs and is known for exploring bold flavors and spices. Among the most popular sauces is Asian Zing, which has a sweet and savory flavor that pairs perfectly with savory fried chicken wings, boneless wings, and vegetarian cauliflower wings. To turn up the heat, stir in a few drops up to 1 teaspoon of your favorite hot sauce.

YIELDS 1 CUP, 2 TABLESPOONS PER SERVING

3/4 cup Thai sweet chili sauce
1 tablespoon light soy sauce
1 tablespoon lemon juice
1 tablespoon rice vinegar
1/2 teaspoon ground ginger

In a small bowl, combine all ingredients. Whisk well and use immediately or transfer to an airtight container and refrigerate up to 7 days.

Air Fryer Buffalo Wings

To make the easiest, nearly mess-free buffalo wings at home, place a single layer of chicken drums and flats in the basket of an air fryer. Air-fry at 400°F 12 minutes, then flip and air-fry another 10–12 minutes until crisp. Toss in your favorite sauce and enjoy!

BUFFALO WILD WINGS HONEY BBQ SAUCE

Typically Served With: Buffalo Wings

When fans of Buffalo Wild Wings talk about their favorite sauces, Honey BBQ Sauce is often at the top of the list. Sweet, tangy, and spicy, this sauce has a lightly smoky flavor that makes it irresistible. The smokiness comes from the addition of a bit of chipotle—or smoked jalapeño pepper—and a bit of smoked paprika. This sauce has a gentle heat that is not overpowering, but you can adjust the sweetness and heat by adding more or less honey and cayenne pepper.

YIELDS 1 CUP, 2 TABLESPOONS PER SERVING

1/2 cup ketchup
1/4 cup honey
2 tablespoons molasses
2 tablespoons apple cider vinegar
1 tablespoon mashed chipotle in adobo
1 tablespoon Dijon mustard
1/2 teaspoon cayenne pepper
1/2 teaspoon smoked paprika
1/2 teaspoon onion powder
1/4 teaspoon garlic powder

1. Place all ingredients in a 2-quart saucepan and mix well. Place over medium heat and bring to a boil, then reduce heat to low and simmer, stirring frequently, 15 minutes.
2. Once sauce has simmered, remove from heat and let cool to room temperature. Use immediately or transfer to an airtight container and refrigerate up to 7 days.

BUFFALO WILD WINGS PARMESAN GARLIC SAUCE

Typically Served With: Buffalo Wings

Creamy, cheesy, and with just the right kiss of spice, Parmesan Garlic Sauce has fans raving about its delicious flavor. It is obviously delicious on chicken wings and boneless wings, but it is also wonderful as a dip for crisp vegetables and a spread for burgers and sandwiches. In fact, in 2025, Buffalo Wild Wings used the sauce on a special March Madness basketball menu sandwich called the Chicken Parm Melt. It featured breaded chicken, mozzarella sticks, pepper jack cheese, marinara sauce, and Parmesan Garlic Sauce spread on a toasted sub roll. That sandwich is sure to fuel game day!

YIELDS 1 CUP, 2 TABLESPOONS PER SERVING

1/2 cup grated Parmesan cheese
1/3 cup mayonnaise
2 tablespoons unsalted butter, softened
1 teaspoon garlic powder
1/2 teaspoon crushed red pepper flakes
1/2 teaspoon onion powder
1/2 teaspoon ground black pepper
1/2 teaspoon Italian seasoning
1/4 teaspoon sea salt

In a medium bowl, whisk together all ingredients until well combined. Use immediately or transfer to an airtight container and refrigerate. Store up to 5 days in the refrigerator. Stir well before use.

BUFFALO WILD WINGS SPICY GARLIC SAUCE

Typically Served With: Buffalo Wings

With a moderate amount of heat—this sauce lands right in the middle of the sauce heat chart—and a bold garlic flavor, Spicy Garlic Sauce is a savory spicy treat for wing lovers. The balance of garlic and spice has fans of this sauce coming back again and again! Fresh garlic gives you the best flavor for this sauce, so the first step is to infuse a small amount of oil with fresh garlic. Be sure to crush the cloves well so the insides are exposed to extract the most flavor.

YIELDS 1 CUP, 2 TABLESPOONS PER SERVING

1/4 cup vegetable oil
4 cloves garlic, peeled and smashed
3/4 cup buffalo wing sauce, such as Frank's RedHot
1 tablespoon mayonnaise
1/4 teaspoon granulated sugar
1/4 teaspoon onion powder
1/4 teaspoon cayenne pepper
1/8 teaspoon garlic powder

1. In a 1-quart saucepan over medium heat, add oil. Once oil is hot and shimmering add garlic and cook, stirring constantly, 1 minute. Remove from heat and let oil and garlic steep 30 minutes.
2. Once steeped, remove and discard garlic. Transfer oil to a bowl, then add remaining ingredients and whisk well. Use immediately or transfer to an airtight container and refrigerate. Store up to 5 days in the refrigerator. Stir well before use.

Easy Blue Cheese Dressing

For a quick blue cheese dressing to enjoy with your buffalo wings, combine 1/2 cup mayonnaise, 1/3 cup blue cheese crumbles, 1/4 cup low-fat buttermilk, and 1/4 teaspoon each sea salt, ground black pepper, and Worcestershire sauce. Mix well and chill 2 hours before serving.

DAIRY QUEEN HARD CHOCOLATE TOPPING

Typically Served With: Ice Cream

Dairy Queen calls their Chocolate Dipped Cone a classic, and they are right! The crunchy chocolate shell and creamy soft serve ice cream served in a sweet cake cone is one of the most popular and nostalgic treats they offer. The coating, which hardens in seconds once it comes into contact with cold ice cream, is a simple mixture of chocolate and coconut oil, so good ingredients really matter! Use high-quality semisweet chips, not chocolate from a bar. The chips have emulsifiers that help them hold their shape when heated, and those help the coating harden.

YIELDS 1 CUP, 2 TABLESPOONS PER SERVING

1 cup semisweet chocolate chips
3 tablespoons coconut oil

1. In a small microwave-safe bowl, add all ingredients. Microwave on high 30 seconds, then stir. Return bowl to the microwave and continue heating in 20-second bursts, stirring well in between, until sauce is melted. Let sauce cool 3 minutes before serving.
2. Leftover sauce can be stored at room temperature up to 5 days. To reheat, microwave in 20-second bursts, stirring well between each, until melted.

What Is the Magic?

Hard-shell ice cream toppings harden because of the addition of coconut oil and/or sunflower oil, both of which harden when chilled. That is why hard-shell ice cream toppings should not be refrigerated, so they can be poured easily. The first hard-shell ice cream toppings were invented in Australia and called Ice Magic.

DAIRY QUEEN HOT FUDGE TOPPING

Typically Served With: Hot Fudge Sundae

Glossy hot fudge sauce may be the most perfect ice cream topping for chocolate fans at Dairy Queen. It remains gooey even on cold ice cream, and it can be used in a simple hot fudge sundae or drizzled over a banana split. Or if you mix it with some roasted peanuts and serve it over vanilla ice cream, you have the DQ Peanut Buster Parfait. Corn syrup is the secret to this glossy sauce, and it keeps the sauce smooth. Without it, the sugar in the sauce could crystallize, so don't leave it out or swap it for honey or agave syrup.

YIELDS 1⅓ CUPS, 2 TABLESPOONS PER SERVING

½ cup granulated sugar
½ cup unsweetened Dutch-processed cocoa powder
½ cup half-and-half
2 tablespoons light corn syrup
¼ cup unsalted butter
1 teaspoon vanilla extract
⅛ teaspoon sea salt

1. In a 2-quart saucepan, combine sugar, cocoa powder, half-and-half, and corn syrup. Whisk well, then heat over medium heat and bring to a boil, about 5 minutes. Boil 3 minutes, then remove pot from heat and whisk in butter, vanilla, and salt.
2. Cool 5 minutes before serving. Leftover sauce can be transferred to an airtight container and stored in the refrigerator up to 7 days. Reheat sauce in a saucepan over low heat until melted.

Origins of the Hot Fudge Sundae

While no one is exactly sure, most believe that before moving from downtown Los Angeles to its famous Hollywood location, C.C. Brown's ice cream parlor sold the first hot fudge sundae when operator Clarence Clifton Brown served a scoop of vanilla ice cream with a pitcher of hot fudge sauce. Customers have loved the hot and cold combo since, making it an instant classic!

DAIRY QUEEN STRAWBERRY TOPPING

Typically Served With: Strawberry Sundae

For Dairy Queen fans who love a refreshing ice cream topping, the Strawberry Topping is a favorite. It is featured in TikTok and Instagram reels from DQ workers showing fun ways it can be blended into Blizzards—such as the Dipped Strawberry Cheesecake Blizzard Treat—or spooned over sundaes. With chunks of real strawberry and a bright red color, it is as pretty to look at as it is enjoyable to eat, making it perfect for showing off on your own social media accounts! The bright red color in this sauce is enhanced with red food coloring, but you can leave it out if you prefer.

YIELDS 1 CUP, 2 TABLESPOONS PER SERVING

½ cup water
2 cups sliced strawberries, divided
½ cup granulated sugar
2 tablespoons cornstarch
1 teaspoon fresh-squeezed lemon juice
2 drops red gel food coloring

1. In a 2-quart saucepan over medium heat, add water and 1 cup strawberries. Mix well and cook, stirring often, until berries release their juice and start to boil. Remove from heat and strain liquid into a heatproof bowl. Discard solids.
2. Return juice to pot and whisk in sugar and cornstarch. Stir in remaining strawberries and heat over medium heat until mixture comes to a boil and sauce thickens, about 5 minutes. Remove from heat and stir in lemon juice and red food coloring. Cool to room temperature before serving.
3. Transfer leftover topping to an airtight container and store up to 4 days in the refrigerator.

DAIRY QUEEN STRAWBERRY TOPPING

DICKEY'S BARBECUE PIT ORIGINAL BBQ SAUCE

Typically Served With: Smoked Brisket

In 1967, Roland and T.D. Dickey took control of the family barbecue restaurant from their father, Travis, and made a commitment to grow the chain without compromising quality and service. This commitment grew a new generation of loyal fans in over 850 locations across forty-four US states and worldwide. Aside from perfectly smoked briskets and ham and irresistible sides, fans love Dickey's Original BBQ Sauce. The flavor is sweet and spicy, with a distinct molasses flavor. It has the right mix of sweet and spicy to complement but not overpower barbecued or smoked meats. This is great on beef, pork, or chicken!

YIELDS 1 CUP, 2 TABLESPOONS PER SERVING

1 cup ketchup
3/4 cup packed dark brown sugar
1/4 cup apple cider vinegar
3 tablespoons molasses
3 tablespoons water
2 teaspoons yellow mustard
1 teaspoon smoked paprika
1 teaspoon garlic powder
1 teaspoon onion powder
1 teaspoon sea salt
1/2 teaspoon Worcestershire sauce
1/2 teaspoon ground black pepper
1/2 teaspoon cayenne pepper

1. In a 2-quart saucepan, combine all ingredients and stir well. Heat over medium heat, stirring constantly, until mixture comes to a boil, then reduce heat to low and simmer until sauce reduces by 1/3, about 20 minutes.
2. Remove sauce from heat and cool to room temperature, then transfer to an airtight container and refrigerate 4 hours before serving. Reheat sauce in a saucepan over low heat before serving. Store up to 7 days in the refrigerator.

DIN TAI FUNG HOUSE SPICY SAUCE

Typically Served With: Spicy Wontons

Founded in Taipei, Taiwan, in 1958, Din Tai Fung is known worldwide for their freshly made dumplings, wontons, and noodles. Fans of the chain have taken to social media, where the reels of steamed dumplings, glossy sauces, and fresh side dishes leave fans begging for more! One of the most popular dishes on the menu is their Spicy Wontons coated in their House Spicy Sauce. It is made by pouring hot oil over a bowl of aromatics to infuse and toast the ingredients. It is best eaten fresh and warm, so make this sauce just before you plan to enjoy it.

YIELDS 1/3 CUP, 3 TABLESPOONS PER SERVING

1 teaspoon red chili flakes
3 cloves garlic, peeled and finely minced
1 teaspoon granulated sugar
1/4 teaspoon five spice powder
1/4 teaspoon Sichuan pepper powder
4 tablespoons chili oil
2 tablespoons soy sauce
1 tablespoon rice vinegar
2 tablespoons sliced green onions, green part only

1. In a small heatproof bowl, add chili flakes, garlic, sugar, five spice powder, and Sichuan pepper powder. Set aside.
2. In an 8-inch frying pan, add chili oil. Heat pan over medium heat until oil is hot, 3–5 minutes. Remove pan from heat and pour oil over ingredients in bowl. Ingredients will sizzle.
3. Once sizzling subsides, whisk in remaining ingredients. Serve immediately.

Expert Dumplings

A quick search on social media for Din Tai Fung will usually result in videos of their talented team of dumpling masters quickly pleating, forming, and folding their wide array of dumplings and wontons. On average, each Din Tai Fung location makes ten thousand dumplings per day!

FOGO DE CHÃO CHIMICHURRI SAUCE

Typically Served With: Steak

In 1979, Fogo de Chão, translating to "Ground Fire," was founded in Porto Alegre, Brazil, offering spit-roasted meats served by gauchos (servers dressed as Brazilian cowboys) and a large buffet-style salad bar featuring cured meats, salads, and soups. The founders wanted to bring Brazil's warm hospitality and delicious food to a new audience, debuting Fogo de Chão in the US in 1997, and today they have over sixty locations globally. While famous for their roasted meats, they also make a popular version of chimichurri sauce that fans love for drizzling and dunking! This version includes a bit of sweet pepper and lots of fresh garlic.

YIELDS 1 CUP, 2 TABLESPOONS PER SERVING

4 cloves garlic, peeled and finely chopped
1 cup lightly packed whole fresh flat leaf parsley leaves, chopped
2 tablespoons finely chopped red bell pepper
1/2 cup extra-virgin olive oil
2 tablespoons white wine vinegar
1/2 teaspoon dried oregano
1/2 teaspoon crushed red pepper flakes
1/2 teaspoon sea salt

Combine all ingredients in a medium bowl and mix well. Transfer to an airtight container and refrigerate 2 hours before serving. Store up to 2 days in the refrigerator.

FIRST WATCH HOLLANDAISE SAUCE

Typically Served With: Classic Benedict

Hollandaise sauce is a thick blend of egg yolks, butter, and seasonings that is a staple of breakfast and brunch restaurants when spooned over eggs Benedict. At First Watch, Benedicts are popular menu items with three different versions on offer besides the Classic Benedict. This sauce is made in a blender to ensure it's nearly foolproof. Timing is important when serving hollandaise sauce, but you can store it for about 10 minutes in a heated thermos or insulated cup. Before making the sauce, pour boiling water in an insulated cup with a lid and let stand 5 minutes, then pour water out and dry well. Once the sauce is ready, transfer it to the cup and cover with a lid.

SERVES 4

½ cup unsalted butter
3 large egg yolks
1 tablespoon fresh lemon juice
1 teaspoon Dijon mustard
⅛ teaspoon sea salt
⅛ teaspoon cayenne pepper

1. In a glass measuring cup, add butter. Microwave 1 minute or until completely melted and very hot.
2. While butter is melting, add remaining ingredients to a blender. Once butter is ready, turn blender on high and pour a slow, steady stream of butter in blender until sauce is thick, 30–45 seconds. Serve immediately.

Healthier Hollandaise Alternative

If you are looking for a healthier alternative to traditional hollandaise, try this! In a small microwave-safe bowl, add ½ cup Greek yogurt, 1 teaspoon fresh lemon juice, 1 teaspoon Dijon mustard, and 1 tablespoon chopped chives. Stir to combine, then microwave on high 15 seconds. Stir well, then heat 10–20 seconds more until sauce is warm. Enjoy!

FIRST WATCH LEMON CURD

Typically Served With: Lemon Ricotta Pancakes

For lovers of creamy and tangy, First Watch Lemon Ricotta Pancakes are the perfect breakfast! Lemon curd is a cooked mixture of sugar, eggs, and butter. It is rich, tangy, and perfect for pancakes or toast or added to desserts. Yes, you can buy lemon curd at the store, but this version has a fresher flavor, and it keeps for up to a week in the refrigerator to enjoy all week long! Pair it with IHOP Original Buttermilk Pancakes or spread it on KFC Biscuits—both recipes are found in Chapter 10—for a special treat!

YIELDS 1 CUP, 2 TABLESPOONS PER SERVING

½ cup fresh lemon juice
½ cup granulated sugar
⅓ cup unsalted butter, cubed and chilled
2 large eggs, at room temperature
1 tablespoon lemon zest
⅛ teaspoon sea salt

1. In a 2-quart saucepan, add all ingredients. Heat over medium-low heat, whisking constantly, until mixture thickens and starts to bubble, 8–10 minutes.
2. Remove pot from heat and pour through a strainer into a medium bowl. Press a piece of plastic wrap directly over bowl and refrigerate 6 hours before serving. Store up to 7 days in the refrigerator.

Copycat Lemon Ricotta Pancakes

Add ½ cup whole milk ricotta cheese to a medium bowl. With a hand mixer, beat on high speed until light and fluffy. Spread half the mixture on a warm pancake (such as from the recipe for IHOP Original Buttermilk Pancakes in Chapter 10), lay a second pancake over ricotta, and spoon a generous dollop of First Watch Lemon Curd on top. Repeat with two additional pancakes. Enjoy!

HOOTERS DAYTONA BEACH SAUCE

Typically Served With: Daytona Beach Style Wings

In 2013, Hooters introduced a new style of chicken wings that differed from the original in that they were not breaded. Called Naked Wings, these new wings were offered fried, smothered in Daytona Beach Sauce, and then grilled. These wings were a hit with fans, who loved the new style of chicken wings and the new sweet and tangy sauce. This sauce is a little thicker than usual wing sauce since it is meant to be brushed over the freshly fried wings before grilling. The sauce can also be used as a glaze for grilled chicken breast, turkey cutlets, or pork chops.

YIELDS 1 CUP, 2 TABLESPOONS PER SERVING

3/4 cup barbecue sauce
1/2 cup Hooters Mild Buffalo Sauce (see recipe in this chapter)
2 tablespoons honey
1 tablespoon packed dark brown sugar
1/2 teaspoon ground black pepper
1/2 teaspoon garlic powder
1/2 teaspoon onion powder
1/4 teaspoon crushed red pepper flakes
1/8 teaspoon Worcestershire sauce

1. In a 2-quart saucepan, add all ingredients and whisk well to combine. Place over medium heat and bring to a boil, stirring often, then reduce heat to low and simmer until sauce thickens to a glaze consistency, about 10 minutes.
2. Serve immediately or transfer to an airtight container and refrigerate up to 7 days. Heat sauce in a saucepan over low heat until steaming hot before serving.

HOOTERS MILD BUFFALO SAUCE

Typically Served With: Hooters Original Style Wings

In 1983, Hooters was founded in Clearwater, Florida, by six business partners who wanted to open a beach-themed restaurant and bar. None of the partners had any restaurant experience, but that did not stop them, and now Hooters is synonymous with hot wings, cold beers, and—shall we say?—saucy servers! Aside from delicious wings smothered in their famous sauce, they are also known for their commitment to charity. Each year, Hooters raises funds for charities like the Special Olympics, Make-A-Wish Foundation, and American Diabetes Association, among others.

YIELDS 1½ CUPS, ¼ CUP PER SERVING

1 cup unsalted butter, softened
⅓ cup Tabasco sauce
2 tablespoons packed light brown sugar
1 tablespoon chili sauce
2 teaspoons balsamic vinegar
½ teaspoon salt
½ teaspoon paprika
½ teaspoon cayenne pepper

In a medium bowl, add all ingredients. Whisk well to combine. Use immediately or cover and refrigerate up to 7 days. Let sauce come to room temperature before use.

Social Media Guidelines

Hooters has strict guidelines about what servers can post to their social media accounts, including prohibiting posting in uniform outside of working hours. When on shift, servers are asked to be "photo ready" with makeup and hair done and in an approved uniform in case a fan wants a photo with their favorite server!

IHOP BLUEBERRY SYRUP

Typically Served With: Pancakes

IHOP is known for their pancakes, breakfast dishes, and also a variety of tasty lunch and dinner options. When it comes to the pancakes, fans of the chain love them dressed up. From limited-time menu favorites like the Rooty Tooty Fresh 'N Fruity or New York Cheesecake Pancakes to the Original Buttermilk Pancakes, guests can customize them with a variety of flavored syrups available on every table. Blueberry fans agree that IHOP Blueberry Syrup is the best around! If you want, you can make this recipe with real maple syrup, but the texture will be thinner.

YIELDS 1 CUP, 2 TABLESPOONS PER SERVING

1 cup pancake syrup
1 cup fresh blueberries

1. In a 1-quart saucepan over medium heat, combine syrup and blueberries. Cook, stirring often, until mixture comes to a simmer. Reduce heat to low and cook 3–5 minutes until blueberries burst and syrup is dark blue.
2. Remove pan from heat and strain sauce into a clean bottle. Cool to room temperature before serving. Refrigerate leftover syrup up to 7 days. Bring to room temperature before serving.

Real Maple Syrup at IHOP

Most IHOP restaurants sell an array of pancake syrups both plain and flavored, but in Vermont they do things a bit differently. There you will find real Vermont maple syrup available for an extra charge. They started this offer in 2009, and they are the only state that makes the offer.

IHOP BLUEBERRY SYRUP

IHOP BUTTER PECAN SYRUP

Typically Served With: Pancakes

Fans of IHOP love the caddy of flavored syrups available on the table for saucing up their breakfast treats! Butter pecan is a popular flavor thought to originate from the African American foodways of the American South. While butter pecan is best known as a flavor of ice cream, IHOP has transformed it into a sweet topping for pancakes and crepes. This recipe uses fresh pecans that are steeped in the warm syrup and strained. If you prefer, instead of discarding them, you can leave the pecans in the bottle or strain them out and stir them into oatmeal and yogurt.

YIELDS 1 CUP, 2 TABLESPOONS PER SERVING

1 cup pancake syrup
1/4 cup chopped toasted pecans
1/4 teaspoon butter extract
1/4 teaspoon vanilla extract

1. In a 1-quart saucepan over medium heat, combine syrup and pecans. Cook, stirring often, until mixture comes to a simmer. Reduce heat to low and cook 5 minutes or until pecans are very fragrant.
2. Remove pan from heat and let syrup cool to room temperature. Once cool, stir in butter and vanilla extracts, then strain into a clean bottle. Refrigerate leftover syrup up to 7 days. Bring to room temperature before serving.

IHOP CINNAMON SAUCE

Typically Served With: Cinn-A-Stack Pancakes

In 2020, IHOP, in an effort to stay profitable, made some strategic cuts to their menu. The reduced menu made it easier and more efficient for workers to keep fans happy and fed. One casualty of these cuts was the popular Cinna-A-Stack Pancakes. In March 2023, IHOP announced the return of a few menu favorites, including the Cinn-A-Stack Pancakes, and fans rejoiced! This recipe is for the ooey-gooey cinnamon filling spread on the warm pancakes (like from the IHOP Original Buttermilk Pancakes recipe in Chapter 10) before they are stacked and garnished with a cream cheese frosting.

YIELDS 1 CUP, 1/4 CUP PER SERVING

1/2 cup unsalted butter, at room temperature
1/2 cup confectioners' sugar
1 tablespoon ground cinnamon
1 tablespoon heavy whipping cream
1/2 teaspoon vanilla extract

In a medium mixing bowl, combine all ingredients. With a hand mixer, beat mixture on low speed until just combined, then increase speed to high and beat 1 minute or until mixture forms a smooth paste. Serve immediately or transfer to an airtight container and refrigerate up to 7 days. Bring to room temperature before serving.

Easy Cream Cheese Topping

In a medium bowl, add 1/3 cup cream cheese and 1/4 cup unsalted butter, both at room temperature. With a hand mixer, beat on medium speed until well combined, about 30 seconds. Add 1 cup confectioners' sugar and 1/2 teaspoon vanilla extract and beat on low to combine. Serves 4. Enjoy!

IHOP GLAZED STRAWBERRIES

Typically Served With: Strawberry Banana Pancakes

Glossy glazed strawberries are a delicious topping for your favorite pancakes, waffles, or even cakes! At IHOP, you can find their Glazed Strawberries on the Strawberry Banana Pancakes, available every day, or on their limited-time menu favorite New York Cheesecake Pancakes. This simple recipe uses strawberry gelatin for extra strawberry flavor and a bold red color. These are best enjoyed when strawberries are in season and at their sweetest. For more tart off-season fruit, add another tablespoon of sugar and 1/4 teaspoon lemon juice to brighten the flavor.

YIELDS 3 CUPS, 1/3 CUP PER SERVING

3/4 cup water
1/4 cup granulated sugar
3 tablespoons strawberry gelatin, such as Jell-O
2 teaspoons cornstarch
3 cups whole strawberries, stems removed
1/4 teaspoon vanilla extract

1. In a 2-quart saucepan over medium heat, add water, sugar, gelatin, and cornstarch. Whisk well. Bring to a boil, constantly whisking, and cook until thickened, 6–8 minutes.
2. Remove from heat and add strawberries and vanilla. Let cool 5 minutes before serving.
3. Transfer leftovers to an airtight container and refrigerate up to 3 days. If mixture is too thick, warm it in a microwave on high 10–12 seconds until runny.

The Smog Hog

Lots of people love the smell of freshly cooked bacon, but if you live near a 24-hour IHOP in close quarters, say in the East Village of New York City, the smell might just become unbearable! That happened to the residents there, and IHOP's solution was to install an odor buster called the "smog hog" that cost $42,000!

OLIVE GARDEN ALFREDO SAUCE

Typically Served With: Fettuccini Pasta

Did you know that the most popular dish at Olive Garden is not the legendary salad or the buttery breadsticks? The most popular menu item is their Chicken Alfredo! The Olive Garden Alfredo Sauce recipe remains unchanged from their start in 1982. It takes some strategic liberties with the classic Italian sauce that inspired it, with the addition of cream for a velvety texture. It is so beloved that when most Americans think of Alfredo sauce, they immediately conjure images of Olive Garden's Alfredo! Enjoy this with pasta that has a broad shape like the classic fettuccini or a tube shape like penne or rigatoni.

SERVES 4

1 tablespoon unsalted butter
2 teaspoons all-purpose flour
2 cloves garlic, peeled and finely minced
1 cup heavy cream
1/2 teaspoon ground black pepper
1/4 teaspoon sea salt
1/8 teaspoon ground nutmeg
1 cup freshly grated Parmesan cheese

1. In a 10-inch nonstick skillet over medium heat, add butter. Stir constantly until butter melts, then stir in flour and garlic and cook 45 seconds. Reduce heat to low and slowly stir in cream, making sure no lumps of flour remain. You can use a nonmetal whisk to work out any lumps.
2. Increase heat to medium-low and stir in pepper, salt, and nutmeg. Cook until sauce starts to simmer, about 1 minute. Add Parmesan cheese 1/4 cup at a time, stirring until each addition of cheese is melted before adding the next.
3. Remove pan from heat. Serve immediately.

OLIVE GARDEN ALFREDO SAUCE

OLIVE GARDEN MARINARA SAUCE

Typically Served With: Spaghetti

Olive Garden takes their tomatoes very seriously! They use a variety of tomatoes grown by select farmers for flavor and quality. The tomatoes are harvested, washed, and sent off to be packaged within hours to ensure peak freshness. Once processed, bags of plain tomato sauce are sent to Olive Garden restaurants to be transformed by chefs into their Marinara Sauce. The sauce is heated in the restaurants along with a packet of concentrated seasonings and then served hot to customers. This process ensures that customers have a consistent experience and the best possible flavor no matter which location they visit!

YIELDS 2 CUPS, 1/2 CUP PER SERVING

2 tablespoons olive oil
1/3 cup finely chopped white onion
2 cloves garlic, peeled and finely minced
1 tablespoon tomato paste
1 teaspoon dried basil
1/2 teaspoon dried oregano
1 (15-ounce) can crushed tomatoes
1 (15-ounce) can diced tomatoes
1/4 teaspoon ground black pepper
1/4 teaspoon granulated sugar
1/4 teaspoon dried rosemary
1/4 teaspoon crushed red pepper flakes

1. In a 3-quart pot over medium heat, add oil. Once oil is hot and shimmering, add onion and sauté until tender, about 5 minutes. Add garlic and tomato paste. Cook until garlic is very fragrant, about 30 seconds. Add basil and oregano and cook 20 seconds.
2. Stir in remaining ingredients, making sure to scrape bottom of pot to release any brown bits stuck to bottom. Bring to a boil, then reduce heat to low and simmer, stirring often, 20 minutes or until sauce is your desired thickness.
3. Serve immediately or transfer to an airtight container and refrigerate up to 5 days. Reheat on stove over medium-low heat until bubbling, 8–10 minutes, before serving.

PANDA EXPRESS HONEY SESAME SAUCE

Typically Served With: Honey Sesame Chicken Breast

Honey Sesame Chicken Breast first appeared as a limited-time offering on the Panda Express menu in 2013, and its annual return became hotly anticipated by fans. In 2020, those fans were excited to learn that the dish was being added to the menu permanently! This dish features lightly fried chicken breast strips and stir-fried vegetables tossed in a sweet and savory honey sauce. Due to its popularity, Panda Express even offered a merchandise line themed around the Honey Sesame Chicken Breast! You can find items such as a hooded onesie, a blazer, and socks printed with panda faces, chicken legs, honey wands, and green beans.

YIELDS 1 CUP, 2 TABLESPOONS PER SERVING

1/2 cup honey
1/4 cup soy sauce
1/4 cup water
2 tablespoons rice vinegar
2 teaspoons fresh lemon juice
2 teaspoons cornstarch
1/2 teaspoon toasted sesame oil
2 teaspoons toasted sesame seeds

In a 1-quart saucepan over medium heat, add all ingredients and whisk well to combine. Bring to a boil, whisking constantly, 5–8 minutes. Once sauce boils, remove from heat. Use immediately or transfer to an airtight container and refrigerate up to 5 days. Reheat sauce on stove over low heat until warm before serving.

PANDA EXPRESS KUNG PAO SAUCE

Typically Served With: Kung Pao Chicken

When traveling to China, you may not recognize kung pao chicken as it is served in Western countries. The authentic Chinese version, a Szechuan dish, has a more intense spice level and is generally more savory. In contrast, the Western version features a sauce that balances savory flavors with sweetness and a hint of spice. At Panda Express, Kung Pao Chicken is one of the most popular entrées, appealing to those who enjoy a good mix of meat, vegetables, and the crunch of roasted peanuts. This dish has been a menu staple for decades and continues to be a top seller!

YIELDS 1 CUP, 2 TABLESPOONS PER SERVING

1/3 cup water
1/4 cup soy sauce
2 tablespoons granulated sugar
1 teaspoon freshly grated ginger
1 teaspoon freshly grated garlic
1 teaspoon sriracha sauce
1 teaspoon cornstarch
1/2 teaspoon toasted sesame oil
1/4 teaspoon crushed red pepper flakes
1/8 teaspoon white pepper

1. In a 1-quart saucepan over medium heat, add all ingredients and whisk well to combine. Bring to a boil, whisking constantly, 5–8 minutes.
2. Once sauce boils, remove from heat. Use immediately or transfer to an airtight container and refrigerate up to 5 days. Reheat sauce on stove over low heat until warm before serving.

Panda Express . . . in China?

In 2020 there were reports that Panda Express had entered the Chinese market in Yunnan Province, much to the surprise and confusion of Chinese citizens. Days later, it was announced by Panda Express executives that the China restaurant was a fraud! While a staple in the West and parts of Asia, Panda Express has no plans to expand into China.

PANDA EXPRESS ORANGE SAUCE

Typically Served With: The Original Orange Chicken

When most Americans think of Chinese food, they think of fried rice, lo mein, and orange chicken—crisp fried chicken coated in a sweet and tangy orange sauce. While orange chicken is a popular American Chinese food dish, and may be inspired by Chinese tangerine chicken, it is not Chinese! Chef Andy Kao is credited with developing the original recipe for orange chicken while working for Panda Express in Hawaii in 1987. Today, The Original Orange Chicken makes up nearly a third of all sales at Panda Express and is the chain's bestselling menu item!

YIELDS 1 CUP, 2 TABLESPOONS PER SERVING

1 cup orange juice
3 (2-inch) strips orange zest
1 clove garlic, peeled and crushed
3 tablespoons packed light brown sugar
2 tablespoons soy sauce
2 tablespoons rice vinegar
½ teaspoon crushed red pepper flakes
½ teaspoon freshly grated ginger
2 tablespoons water
1 tablespoon cornstarch

1. In a 1-quart saucepan over medium heat, add orange juice and orange zest. Bring to a boil and cook 5 minutes or until reduced by ¼. Reduce heat to low, add remaining ingredients, and stir well to combine.
2. Increase heat to medium and bring sauce back to a boil, stirring constantly, 1–2 minutes. Once sauce boils, remove from heat and strain into a medium bowl. Discard solids. Use immediately or transfer to an airtight container and refrigerate up to 5 days. Reheat sauce on stove over low heat until warm before serving.

A Special Meaning

Panda Express's origins trace back to 1973 when Andrew and Peggy Cherng opened the Panda Inn restaurant in Pasadena, California. The name Panda Inn came from then-President Richard Nixon's 1972 visit to China, with the panda used as a symbol of friendship between the two countries. Panda Express opened their first location in 1983 and today operates over two thousand locations globally!

P.F. CHANG'S TERIYAKI SAUCE

Typically Served With: Teriyaki Beef

P.F. Chang's Teriyaki Sauce is a sweet and salty blend of soy sauce, pineapple juice, brown sugar, and sake that is cooked down and then gently thickened so it can coat stir-fried beef, chicken, or your favorite vegetables. The sake, a Japanese alcoholic beverage, helps give this sauce a clean flavor, and almost all the alcohol will boil off during cooking, but if you are avoiding alcohol, you can substitute an additional 3 tablespoons pineapple juice or water without harm to the overall flavor. You can use this as a finishing sauce, marinade, or glaze for grilled and roasted meats. It is very versatile!

YIELDS 1¼ CUPS SAUCE, 3 TABLESPOONS PER SERVING

½ cup water, divided
⅓ cup soy sauce
¼ cup packed light brown sugar
¼ cup pineapple juice
3 tablespoons sake
1 teaspoon rice vinegar
¼ teaspoon freshly grated ginger
¼ teaspoon freshly grated garlic
2 teaspoons cornstarch

1. In a 2-quart saucepan over medium heat, add all ingredients except cornstarch and 1 tablespoon water. Stir well and bring mixture to a boil, 8–10 minutes.
2. Once mixture is boiling, let cook 5 minutes or until reduced by ¼.
3. Once mixture is reduced, in a small bowl, combine cornstarch with remaining water and mix well. Stir cornstarch mixture into boiling mixture, stirring until sauce thickens, about 30 seconds. Remove pan from heat and serve immediately.
4. Transfer leftover sauce to an airtight container and refrigerate up to 4 days.

Authentic Japanese Teriyaki

In the US, teriyaki sauce is known as a somewhat thick, sweet sauce used as a glaze, but in Japan it is a bit different. Teriyaki refers to a cooking technique of grilling food over fire while glazing it with a mixture of soy sauce, mirin, and sugar until the meat is burnished and glistening. The name comes from *teri,* meaning "gloss" or "luster," and *yaki,* which means "grilled" or "broiled."

PIZZA HUT CINNABON SIGNATURE CREAM CHEESE FROSTING

Typically Served With: Cinnabon Mini Rolls

In 2018, a collaboration was announced that no one in the pizza world saw coming—Pizza Hut and Cinnabon were joining forces to create warm, sweet dessert cinnamon rolls that customers could have delivered directly to their door! Cinnabon Mini Rolls, a box of ten miniature cinnamon rolls served smothered in the chain's popular cream cheese frosting, were added as a permanent menu item, and fans of both Pizza Hut and Cinnabon were thrilled! Fans rushed to social media to share their reviews, often recording themselves tasting the rolls for their followers.

YIELDS 1 CUP, 2 TABLESPOONS PER SERVING

3 ounces cream cheese, at room temperature
¼ cup unsalted butter, at room temperature
1½ cups confectioners' sugar
½ teaspoon pure vanilla extract
⅛ teaspoon salt

1. In a medium bowl, combine cream cheese, butter, confectioners' sugar, vanilla, and salt. With an electric mixer, beat on low 30 seconds to combine ingredients, then increase speed to high and beat 1 minute or until frosting is light and fluffy.
2. Serve immediately or transfer to an airtight container and refrigerate up to 3 days. Allow frosting to come to room temperature before serving.

Easy Cinnamon Twist Dippers

Preheat oven to 375°F and line a baking pan with baking parchment. Roll out 1 tube (13.8-ounce) refrigerated pizza crust. Brush with 3 tablespoons melted unsalted butter, then sprinkle ¼ cup packed dark brown sugar mixed with ½ teaspoon ground cinnamon over dough. Fold dough in half, cut into 1-inch-wide strips, twist, and place on prepared baking sheet. Bake 10–12 minutes until golden brown. Cool 3 minutes before serving.

PIZZA HUT CINNABON SIGNATURE CREAM CHEESE FROSTING

RED ROBIN BUZZARD SAUCE

Typically Served With: Chicken Wings

Also known as Buzz Sauce, Buzzard Sauce is Red Robin's classic buffalo wing sauce, and it has a tangy flavor with a bit of heat. The sauce has a unique flavor compared to other wing sauces, largely due to the amount of Worcestershire sauce added. It gives the sauce a depth of flavor and extra tang that fans find irresistible! Aside from tossing with wings, you can use this as a marinade for grilled or fried chicken, or mix ½ cup ranch with ¼ cup Buzzard Sauce to make a buffalo ranch dressing for your favorite salad or use as a dip for crisp carrot and celery sticks.

YIELDS 1 CUP, 2 TABLESPOONS PER SERVING

¾ cup hot pepper sauce, such as Tabasco
3 tablespoons Worcestershire sauce
1 teaspoon garlic powder
¼ teaspoon cayenne pepper

Combine all ingredients in a medium bowl and mix well. Transfer to an airtight container and refrigerate 2 hours before serving. Store up to 7 days in the refrigerator.

RED ROBIN ISLAND HEAT SAUCE

Typically Served With: Chicken Wings

Red Robin describes their Island Heat Sauce as a "heat meets sweet sauce," making it the perfect choice for those who enjoy a sweet and savory flavor for their wings without sacrificing a spicy kick. The fan favorite tropical flavors come from fresh mango and pineapple juice blended into the sauce. If you can't find regular habanero pepper powder, you can substitute Tajín Habanero Seasoning or blend in half a seeded fresh habanero pepper. Keep in mind that the heat level of fresh peppers can vary, so feel free to add more if you want a spicier kick!

YIELDS 1 CUP, 2 TABLESPOONS PER SERVING

1/2 cup ketchup
1/4 cup mango chunks
2 tablespoons pineapple juice
1 tablespoon packed light brown sugar
1/2 teaspoon garlic powder
1/2 teaspoon onion powder
1/4 teaspoon habanero pepper powder

Combine all ingredients in a blender and purée until smooth, about 1 minute. Transfer to an airtight container and refrigerate 4 hours before serving. Store up to 4 days in the refrigerator.

RUTH'S CHRIS STEAK HOUSE BUTTER

Typically Served With: Steak

Ruth's Chris Steak House is well-known for its delicious sizzling steaks with their signature caramelized crust. They prepare their steaks using an infrared broiler that quickly sears and browns the steaks. When they come out of the broiler, the steaks are placed on heated plates and topped with a delicious compound butter that melts, sizzles, and browns on the plate, adding an extra layer of flavor. A compound butter is butter mixed with other ingredients and used for cooking or finishing a hot dish. You can use this butter on steaks or grilled or roasted chicken or as a topping for grilled fish and seafood.

YIELDS 1 CUP, 1 TABLESPOON PER SERVING

1 cup unsalted butter, at room temperature
2 cloves garlic, peeled and finely minced
1 tablespoon fresh chopped parsley leaves
½ teaspoon sea salt
¼ teaspoon ground black pepper
¼ teaspoon Worcestershire sauce

1. In a medium bowl, add all ingredients. With a spatula or wooden spoon, mix to combine ingredients well.
2. Lay a 10" ×10" square of baking parchment on a work surface. Transfer butter mixture to center of paper and roughly form a log shape about 6 inches long. Fold paper over long side of butter log, and with your hand, press against side of log. Roll paper around log and twist ends until butter forms a tight, even log.
3. Refrigerate butter 4 hours before serving. Store up to 5 days in the refrigerator.

Ruth's Chris Early History

In 1965, Ruth Fertel mortgaged her home to buy Chris Steak House in New Orleans. Although she knew little about the restaurant business, she quickly learned and even designed their proprietary 1,800°F broiler. Unfortunately, the original steak house burned down in 1976, and Ruth's contract prevented her from using the name for her new location. She improvised and decided to add her name, and Ruth's Chris Steak House was born!

SNOOZE, AN A.M. EATERY SMOKED CHEDDAR HOLLANDAISE

Typically Served With: Ham Benedict III

In 2006, two Denver, Colorado, brothers, Adam and Jon Schlegel, opened the first Snooze, an A.M. Eatery to change the breakfast game. Their recipes offer fun twists on breakfast classics while keeping the community and the planet in mind. They hope each guest will clean their plates, but when they don't, Snooze composts and recycles up to 90 percent of their kitchen waste. They also work to purchase their ingredients and supplies from sustainable sources and partner with people who share their values toward the environment. Best of all, they donate 1 percent of their sales back to the communities they serve!

SERVES 4

1/2 cup unsalted butter
3 large egg yolks
1 tablespoon fresh lemon juice
1 teaspoon Dijon mustard
1/8 teaspoon sea salt
1/8 teaspoon smoked paprika
1/2 ounce freshly fine-grated smoked Cheddar cheese, at room temperature

1. In a glass measuring cup, add butter. Microwave 1 minute or until completely melted and very hot.
2. While butter is melting, add eggs, lemon juice, mustard, salt, and paprika to a blender. Once butter is melted, turn blender on high and pour a slow, steady stream of butter in blender until sauce is thick, 30–45 seconds. When all butter is added, add cheese and purée 10–15 seconds more. Serve immediately.

SNOOZE, AN A.M. EATERY VANILLA CREAM SAUCE

Typically Served With: OMG! French Toast

Sometimes social media has less to do with one viral moment and more to do with virtual word-of-mouth success! When you see friends and family posting about their favorite places, showcasing unique meals in a fun environment, it becomes hard to resist checking those places out. This is a key part of Snooze, an A.M. Eatery's success. Fans of the chain love to share their favorite meals, showing off the unique breakfast creations they love most. One standout feature is a delicious Vanilla Cream Sauce that accompanies several pancake and French toast offerings. It is sweet and creamy and can be used for dressing fresh berries or drizzling over cake slices.

YIELDS 1 CUP, 2 TABLESPOONS PER SERVING

1/4 cup confectioners' sugar
2 teaspoons vanilla extract
1 teaspoon water
3/4 teaspoon cornstarch
1 cup heavy whipping cream

1. In a small bowl, combine confectioners' sugar, vanilla, water, and cornstarch and mix to form a smooth paste. Set aside.
2. In a 1-quart saucepan over medium heat, add cream. Heat, stirring often, until cream starts to simmer, about 5 minutes. Whisk in confectioners' sugar mixture and continue to cook, stirring constantly, until cream thickens and can coat the back of a spoon thickly.
3. Remove mixture from heat and serve immediately or transfer to an airtight container and refrigerate up to 3 days. Reheat sauce on stove over low heat until warm before serving.

WHATABURGER HONEY BUTTER SAUCE

Typically Served With: Honey Butter Chicken Biscuit

If you ask country music star Lainey Wilson, named a Whataburger spokesperson in 2025, the Whataburger Honey Butter Chicken Biscuit sandwich is so good, if she were on death row she would make it her last meal! Fans of the breakfast sandwich—which started, as so many menu mainstays at Whataburger do, as a limited-time offer—particularly love the Honey Butter Sauce that is drizzled over the chicken. The sandwich is only available for breakfast, but with this sauce recipe you can enjoy that flavor all day long! The sauce is also excellent on sweet rolls, pancakes, French toast, and so much more.

YIELDS 1 CUP, 2 TABLESPOONS PER SERVING

1/4 cup unsalted butter, melted and cooled
1/4 cup liquid margarine, such as Parkay
3 tablespoons honey
1/4 teaspoon white vinegar
1/4 teaspoon sea salt

Combine all ingredients in a blender and purée until smooth, about 1 minute. Transfer to an airtight container and refrigerate 4 hours before serving. Store up to 7 days in the refrigerator. Warm in the microwave on high 20–30 seconds until just melted before serving.

Corpus Christi Honey Butter Chicken Biscuits Baseball

The Corpus Christi Hooks, a minor league baseball team that is the Double-A affiliate team for the Houston Astros, had a different name on Wednesdays back in 2021. They would break out orange and white uniforms emblazoned with the name Corpus Christi Honey Butter Chicken Biscuits in honor of the town where the chain got its start!

WINGSTOP GARLIC PARMESAN WING SAUCE

Typically Served With: Classic Bone-In Wings

Not all wings need to be screaming hot or a test of your tolerance for heat to be enjoyable. Plenty of mild sauces offer delicious flavor without the burn. Wingstop has perfected this with their mild but flavor-packed Garlic Parmesan Wing Sauce. It is a blend of garlic, parsley, black pepper, Parmesan cheese, and butter that fans absolutely adore! This sauce calls for clarified butter (see sidebar for a quick recipe), but ghee is a good substitute if you prefer. You can also add some heat by adding ½ teaspoon crushed red pepper in with the garlic at the beginning of this recipe.

YIELDS ¾ CUP, 2 TABLESPOONS PER SERVING

½ cup clarified butter, melted, divided
2 cloves garlic, peeled and finely minced
¼ teaspoon ground black pepper
¼ teaspoon dried parsley
¼ teaspoon garlic powder
¼ cup freshly grated Parmesan cheese

1. In a 1-quart saucepan, add 2 tablespoons clarified butter. Heat over medium heat until shimmering, then add garlic and sauté 30 seconds or until very fragrant. Remove from heat and add remaining clarified butter, pepper, parsley, and garlic powder. Use immediately, sprinkling Parmesan cheese as a garnish.
2. If not using right away, transfer to an airtight container and refrigerate up to 3 days. Heat sauce before using.

Clarified Butter

Add 2 sticks of unsalted butter, cut into tablespoon-sized pieces, to a microwave-safe glass measuring cup. Microwave on high 1–2 minutes until butter starts to bubble. Let stand 2 minutes. Butter should form a clear yellow layer with a milky layer on bottom. Spoon off any solids on top, then carefully pour the clear layer in a jar for storage. Discard bottom layer. Refrigerate up to 6 months.

CHAPTER 9

~~DON'T~~ FILL UP ON DIP: HEARTY DIPS

Looking for an appetizer or party dip to please a crowd? Craving a dinner of chips and dips? Need something tasty and fun to take to a potluck or progressive dinner? This chapter has just what you are looking for! Here you will find delicious, hearty dips and fun fondues that are as enjoyable to make as they are to eat. If you are looking for an interactive dinner where family and friends can talk, eat, and play with their food, you will want to make The Melting Pot Wisconsin Cheddar Fondue or Spinach Artichoke Fondue. You can even end the night on a sweet note with The Melting Pot Original Chocolate Fondue. Craving tortilla chips dunked in rich, cheesy queso? Torchy's Tacos Green Chile Queso or On The Border Mexican Grill & Cantina Signature Queso are both tasty and satisfying options. Maybe Mediterranean is what you crave? CAVA Red Pepper Hummus or Tzatziki should be on the menu. Artichoke fans can make a hearty dip for spooning onto toasted bread, such as the Applebee's Neighborhood Grill + Bar Spinach & Artichoke Dip or Ruth's Chris Steakhouse Goat Cheese & Artichoke Dip. Finding the perfect hearty dip is easy with recipes this good!

APPLEBEE'S NEIGHBORHOOD GRILL + BAR SPINACH & ARTICHOKE DIP

Typically Served With: Tortilla Chips

While most spinach and artichoke dips are made with a base that is often a mix of cream cheese and either mayonnaise or sour cream, this dip skips those heavier ingredients and starts with a base more closely related to an American-style Alfredo sauce. Fans of this classic dip frequently cite it as a favorite appetizer because of the ratio of vegetables to creamy, cheesy sauce. It is the ultimate comfort food appetizer, and when paired with warm tortilla chips (like the Chipotle Chips in Chapter 10), it will be sure to become a favorite from your own kitchen!

SERVES 6

2 tablespoons unsalted butter
2 tablespoons vegetable oil
4 cups lightly packed chopped baby spinach
1 (13.75-ounce) can quartered artichoke hearts in brine, drained, rinsed, and chopped
1 clove garlic, peeled and minced
½ teaspoon onion powder
3 tablespoons all-purpose flour
1 cup whole milk
½ cup heavy whipping cream
½ cup freshly grated Asiago cheese
½ cup freshly grated Parmesan cheese

1. Preheat oven to 375°F and spray an 8" × 8" square pan with nonstick cooking spray.
2. In a 2-quart saucepan over medium heat, add butter and oil. Once butter is melted, add spinach and cook until spinach is fully wilted, about 3 minutes. Stir in artichoke hearts, garlic, and onion powder and cook 1 minute.
3. Reduce heat to medium-low and add flour. Stir well to combine flour and cook 2 minutes. Slowly add milk, stirring constantly to work out any lumps, then stir in cream. Increase heat to medium and cook, stirring constantly, until mixture starts to bubble and thicken, about 5 minutes.
4. Reduce heat to low and stir in Asiago cheese. Once cheese is melted, transfer mixture to prepared dish and top with Parmesan cheese. Bake 15–20 minutes until dip is bubbling hot around edges and cheese on top has browned. Cool 5 minutes before serving. Enjoy warm.

APPLEBEE'S NEIGHBORHOOD GRILL + BAR WHITE QUESO DIP

Typically Served With: Tortilla Chips

Queso, a Tex-Mex-style cheese dip, is one of the most popular appetizers and party dips among Americans. Served with warm tortilla chips, it does not get much better! At Applebee's, the queso is made from mild and creamy white American cheese and studded with fresh pico de gallo. The tomatoes, onions, and peppers add freshness and a bright flavor to the dip, making it hard to stop eating! Here we use the Moe's Southwest Grill Pico de Gallo recipe in Chapter 2, but you can use store-bought or another favorite recipe if you prefer.

SERVES 6

1 cup half-and-half
8 ounces white deli American cheese, chopped
1 tablespoon pickled jalapeño brine
½ cup prepared Moe's Southwest Grill Pico de Gallo (Chapter 2)

1. In a 2-quart saucepan, add half-and-half. Heat over medium-low heat until half-and-half starts to steam, 2–3 minutes. Add half American cheese and whisk until cheese is fully melted, then add remaining cheese and whisk until smooth, about 3 minutes.
2. Reduce heat to low and whisk in jalapeño brine, then fold in pico de gallo. Serve immediately.

Queso Variations

Here are a few ways to dress up your next batch of queso to change up the flavors. Make it hearty and add ⅓ cup prepared taco meat just before serving. Give it a Southwest vibe and swap the pico de gallo for one can of drained Hatch diced green chilies. To add more spice, stir in ½–1 teaspoon of your favorite hot pepper sauce.

BAHAMA BREEZE CRAB AND THREE CHEESE DIP

Typically Served With: Tortilla Chips

Tender lump crabmeat and three cheeses baked to bubbling golden brown and served warm with tortilla chips? Yes, please! Bahama Breeze fans rave about their cheesy crab dip because it is loaded with flavor and perfect for those who love a rich, cheesy seafood-studded starter. Crabmeat is generally sold in vacuum-sealed cans at your grocery store's seafood department in a refrigerated case. Lump crabmeat is usually the most expensive available, so if you are looking to save a little money, you can swap it for claw meat or even imitation crabmeat.

SERVES 4

4 ounces cream cheese, softened
1/4 cup sour cream
2 tablespoons mayonnaise
1 teaspoon fresh lemon juice
1/2 teaspoon Tabasco sauce
1/2 teaspoon Worcestershire sauce
1/2 teaspoon Old Bay seasoning
1/2 teaspoon onion powder
1/4 teaspoon garlic powder
1/4 teaspoon ground black pepper
4 ounces lump crabmeat
1/2 cup shredded sharp Cheddar cheese
1/4 cup freshly grated Parmesan cheese

1. Preheat oven to 350°F and spray a 6-inch baking dish or cast iron dish with nonstick cooking spray.
2. In a medium bowl, combine cream cheese, sour cream, and mayonnaise. With a hand mixer on medium speed, beat until combined and smooth, about 2 minutes. Add lemon juice, Tabasco, Worcestershire sauce, Old Bay, onion powder, garlic powder, and pepper and mix on low to combine, about 30 seconds.
3. Scrape sides of bowl down with spatula, then add crabmeat and Cheddar cheese and fold to combine. Transfer mixture to prepared dish and top with Parmesan cheese.
4. Bake 20–25 minutes until dip is bubbling around edges and cheese on top is golden brown. Cool 5 minutes before serving. Serve warm.

Maryland Origins

The crab dip that most people enjoy is believed to have originated in Maryland, where blue crab fishing has traditionally been a big industry. The dip usually combines ingredients like mayonnaise and/or cream cheese along with vegetables, spices, and plenty of lump crab.

BUBBA GUMP SHRIMP CO. BUBBA'S FAR OUT DIP

Typically Served With: Tortilla Chips

When Bubba Gump Shrimp Co. calls this dip "far out," they are not kidding! It is their take on spinach artichoke dip, but this version has more vegetables and less creamy cheese base, which makes it different. The key to some of that "far out" flavor is the pimentos. They add a sweet, earthy flavor that balances the savory artichokes and cheese. At the restaurant, you can order the dip with shrimp, and you can have it that way at home too. Once all the ingredients are combined, fold in ½ cup chopped cooked shrimp and bake as directed.

SERVES 6

1 (13.75-ounce) can quartered artichoke hearts, drained and chopped
8 ounces frozen chopped spinach, thawed and drained
4 ounces cream cheese, at room temperature
½ cup grated Monterey jack cheese
¼ cup freshly grated Parmesan cheese
¼ cup mayonnaise
1 (4-ounce) jar pimentos, drained
½ medium red onion, peeled and finely chopped
½ teaspoon ground black pepper
½ teaspoon garlic powder
¼ teaspoon paprika

1. Preheat oven to 350°F and spray an 8" × 8" baking dish with nonstick cooking spray.
2. In a medium bowl, combine artichoke hearts, spinach, cream cheese, Monterey jack cheese, Parmesan cheese, and mayonnaise. Once well mixed, add remaining ingredients and fold to combine.
3. Transfer dip to prepared baking dish, cover with aluminum foil, and bake 20 minutes, uncover and bake 10 minutes more or until dip is hot and bubbling around edges. Cool 5 minutes before serving. Serve warm.

CALIFORNIA PIZZA KITCHEN MEXICAN STREET CORN

Typically Served With: Grilled Bread

Mexican street corn is an incredibly popular street food dish sold either on the cob or in cups. California Pizza Kitchen serves their elevated version of this dish with slices of grilled bread and garnished with tangy feta cheese. To make the dip easier to prepare, this recipe calls for frozen fire-roasted corn. It should be prepared as per the package directions so it is hot when the dip is mixed. If you do not have a package available, you can roast fresh corn. Directions can be found in the sidebar.

SERVES 6

1 (12-ounce) package frozen fire-roasted corn, such as Birds Eye, prepared per package directions
1/4 cup plus 2 tablespoons crumbled feta cheese, divided
2 tablespoons freshly grated Parmesan cheese
2 tablespoons ranch dressing
2 tablespoons mayonnaise
1 teaspoon hot pepper sauce, such as Tabasco
1 tablespoon minced fresh cilantro
2 teaspoons fresh lime juice

In a medium bowl, combine all ingredients except 2 tablespoons feta and mix until well combined. Serve immediately garnished with remaining feta.

Making Fire-Roasted Corn

Brush six ears of fresh shucked yellow or sweet corn with 1 tablespoon vegetable oil. Heat grill to medium-high heat. Grill corn cobs, turning often, until kernels are soft and lightly charred, about 15 minutes. Let corn cool slightly before cutting off kernels and proceed with the recipe as written.

CAVA CRAZY FETA

Typically Served With: Spicy Chicken + Avocado Pita

Ted Xenohristos, Ike Grigoropoulos, and Dimitri Moshovitis opened Cava Mezze in Rockville, Maryland, as a full-service Mediterranean restaurant. The restaurant evolved into a fast-casual concept and rebranded as CAVA by 2011, and in 2018 the partnership, which had added members, purchased rival Zoë's Kitchen to become the largest Mediterranean restaurant operator in the United States. They are best known for fresh ingredients, bold flavors, recipes made with simple ingredients, and an array of house-made dips and spreads. Crazy Feta is one of the most popular dips they offer, and it is made simply with fresh feta cheese and olive oil whipped, then mixed with sautéed onion and jalapeño.

YIELDS 1¼ CUPS, 2 TABLESPOONS PER SERVING

8 ounces crumbled feta cheese
¼ cup extra-virgin olive oil, divided
¼ cup chopped jalapeño
¼ cup chopped yellow onion

1. In a food processor, add feta and 3 tablespoons oil. Process on high, scraping sides of bowl down occasionally, until feta is smooth and creamy, about 3 minutes. Transfer to a medium bowl with an airtight lid and set aside.
2. In an 8-inch skillet over medium heat, add remaining oil. Once oil is hot, add jalapeño and onion and sauté until tender, 3–5 minutes. Remove from heat and let cool 5 minutes before adding to feta and folding to combine.
3. Cover bowl with lid and refrigerate 4 hours before serving. Store up to 4 days in the refrigerator. Serve dip at room temperature.

Crazy Tasty

Crazy Feta was created by Dimitri Moshovitis, also known as Chef D, who is one of CAVA's founders. In 2006 he was working in the kitchen on new recipes, largely inspired by his Greek heritage and watching his mother cook when he was young. Looking to share family recipes with a fun twist, he made a test batch of whipped feta but added vegetables sautéed in olive oil for a new take on the classic. One of the cooks tasted it and exclaimed, "It's crazy!" Chef D knew that had to be the name, thus Crazy Feta was born!

CAVA CRAZY FETA

CAVA HARISSA

Typically Served With: Bowls

Harissa is a North African condiment made with a spice blend composed of chili peppers, garlic, olive oil, and other spices. CAVA Harissa is a thick dip that starts with tomato, giving it a tangy sweetness that complements the spices and garlic. It is served as a dip, but it can also be used as a spread or condiment for wraps and bowls. You can find ground harissa spice blends at most grocery stores or online. This dip starts with 1 tablespoon, but you can add more to amp up the flavor, or toss in some other ground spicy chili pepper powders to increase the spice factor!

YIELDS 1 CUP, 2 TABLESPOONS PER SERVING

1 (6-ounce) can tomato paste
2/3 cup water
3 tablespoons extra-virgin olive oil
1 tablespoon harissa, such as Morton & Bassett
1 tablespoon dried parsley
1/2 teaspoon sea salt
1/2 teaspoon onion powder
1/2 teaspoon garlic powder
1/2 teaspoon fresh lemon juice

1. In a 2-quart saucepan, combine all ingredients and whisk until smooth. Heat mixture over medium heat and cook, stirring often, until it comes to a simmer, about 5 minutes. Reduce heat to low and let mixture simmer, stirring often, until it thickens, 8–10 minutes.
2. Transfer to an airtight container and refrigerate 4 hours before serving. Store up to 7 days in the refrigerator. Serve at room temperature.

Harissa on Social Media

Harissa has found some popularity on social media in recipes and among health and lifestyle influencers who tout its anti-inflammatory benefits along with its delicious flavor. Most popular among the viral recipes are those for harissa with beans, harissa chicken, and harissa pasta.

CAVA RED PEPPER HUMMUS

Typically Served With: Steak + Feta Pita

CAVA is one of the fastest-growing restaurant brands in the United States, gaining new fans every day. They love the fast-casual atmosphere, the fresh foods, the delicious flavors, and CAVA's commitment to their teams and the community. They are also committed to good food that does not sacrifice quality or freshness and uses time-tested recipes while not shying away from innovation. This recipe is for a simple yet flavor-packed roasted red pepper hummus that relies on tahini and roasted red pepper for a big flavor impact. The addition of a bit of chia seeds helps this hummus have a richer, thicker texture after resting.

YIELDS 1 CUP, 2 TABLESPOONS PER SERVING

1 can (15.5 ounces) chickpeas, drained and rinsed
½ cup chopped jarred roasted red pepper
¼ cup tahini
1 clove garlic, peeled
½ teaspoon ground cumin
½ teaspoon sea salt
½ teaspoon chia seeds

1. Place drained chickpeas on a clean kitchen towel and rub them gently to remove the skins. Discard skins and place chickpeas in a food processor.
2. Combine remaining ingredients in food processor with chickpeas. Purée, scraping down sides of blender occasionally until mixture is smooth, about 2 minutes. If hummus is too thick, add a little water a tablespoon at a time until it thins to your preference.
3. Transfer to an airtight container and refrigerate 4 hours before serving. Store up to 7 days in the refrigerator.

CAVA TRADITIONAL HUMMUS

Typically Served With: Crispy Falafel Pita

CAVA is happy to let you know that their hummus dips do not use any oil, making them stand out from most hummus recipes out there. The richness of this dip comes from tahini—a paste made from sesame seeds—and a little water. One key step to a creamy hummus is to remove the chickpea skins. It is easy to do with canned or cooked chickpeas by gently rubbing them with a towel until the skins come free. Just pluck the now naked chickpeas off the towel and discard the skins. If you choose to skip this step, the only difference is your hummus will be a bit gritty, but it will still taste amazing!

YIELDS 1 CUP, 2 TABLESPOONS PER SERVING

1 (15.5-ounce) can chickpeas, drained and rinsed
1/3 cup tahini
2 tablespoons water
2 cloves garlic, peeled
1 tablespoon fresh lemon juice
1/2 teaspoon sea salt

1. Place drained chickpeas on a clean kitchen towel and rub them gently to remove the skins. Discard skins and place chickpeas in a food processor.
2. Combine remaining ingredients in food processor with chickpeas. Purée, scraping down sides of blender occasionally until mixture is smooth, about 2 minutes. If hummus is too thick, add a little more water a tablespoon at a time until it thins to your preference.
3. Transfer to an airtight container and refrigerate 4 hours before serving. Store up to 7 days in the refrigerator.

CAVA TZATZIKI

Typically Served With: Greek Chicken Pita

Tzatziki is a traditional Mediterranean dip and condiment made with tangy Greek yogurt, cucumber, dill, and a bit of lemon and olive oil. Creamy and refreshing, CAVA Tzatziki is the perfect condiment for their selection of spiced meats like chicken, lamb, or beef. It can also be enjoyed spread on warm pita or used as a dip for crunchy fresh vegetables. It is at its best when it has had a chance to rest, so be sure to give it some chilling time before eating. If you prefer, you can swap the fresh dill with dried dill; just reduce the amount to 2 teaspoons.

YIELDS 1 CUP, 2 TABLESPOONS PER SERVING

3/4 cup plain low-fat Greek yogurt
1/3 cup grated English cucumber, excess liquid wrung out with a clean towel
1 tablespoon chopped fresh dill
2 teaspoons lemon juice
1 teaspoon extra-virgin olive oil
1/2 teaspoon freshly grated garlic
1/4 teaspoon sea salt

In a medium bowl, combine all ingredients and mix well. Cover and refrigerate 4 hours before serving. Store up to 7 days in the refrigerator. Stir well before serving.

Viral Mispronunciation

Rick Wiggins (@ketosnackz on Instagram) has made a name for himself posting reels of keto-friendly recipes where he occasionally, and intentionally, mispronounces something to bait users to respond. In one viral reel he called tzatziki "tee-za-tee-zay-kai," and it spawned hilarious response videos, including one of a trio of comically angry Greek men correcting him.

CHILI'S SKILLET BEEF QUESO

Typically Served With: Tortilla Chips and Fresh Salsa

This queso dip is easy to whip together, taking just 10 minutes of cooking time, and it's sure to please anyone you serve it to! Among the most popular appetizers on Chili's menu, it is a fun twist on the Tex-Mex classic with the addition of chili to the mix. Chili's has claimed that this dip, added to the menu sometime in the early 1990s, sells as many as four million orders each year! At Chili's, Skillet Beef Queso is paired with a serving of Chili's Fresh Salsa (Chapter 2) and a basket of warm, extra-crisp, super-salty tortilla chips for dipping, but it would also make an excellent topping for burgers or hot dogs.

SERVES 6

1 (8-ounce) block Velveeta Original Cheese, cut into 1-inch cubes
½ cup whole milk
1 cup canned no-bean chili, such as Hormel
1 teaspoon chili powder
1 teaspoon paprika
¼ teaspoon ground cumin

1. In a 2-quart saucepan, combine Velveeta and milk. Heat over medium-low heat, stirring constantly, until cheese melts and mixture is smooth, about 5 minutes.
2. Stir in remaining ingredients and continue to cook 3–5 minutes more until dip is hot. Serve immediately.

The Great Bean Debate

Search "chili" online, and you are sure to find people arguing about one hotly contested topic—beans or no beans in chili. Your opinion on this may largely depend on where you are from. Most Texans, for example, say no to beans in chili, while people in the Midwest and West love them!

CHIPOTLE GUACAMOLE

Typically Served With: Tortilla Chips

In 2019, Chipotle Guacamole went viral with their #GuacDance challenge, created to celebrate National Avocado Day. The dance challenge, which featured children's musician Dr. Jean and her guacamole song, had over 250,000 submissions and at the time was the best-performing branded challenge in the United States. What was the result of the challenge? Chipotle sold over 800,000 sides of their Guacamole, a jump of 68 percent! You may wonder, what makes Chipotle Guacamole so good? It is a simple recipe, but the magic is from lightly mashing the aromatic ingredients to release more flavor.

YIELDS 1 CUP, 1/4 CUP PER SERVING

2 tablespoons minced red onion
2 tablespoons chopped fresh cilantro
1 tablespoon minced fresh jalapeño
1 tablespoon fresh lime juice
1/4 teaspoon sea salt
2 large ripe Hass avocados

1. In a medium bowl, add onion, cilantro, jalapeño, lime juice, and salt. With a wooden spoon, gently mash ingredients five or six times or until very fragrant.
2. Slice open avocados, remove pits, and scoop flesh into bowl. With a potato masher, mash until avocado is mostly smooth with some small chunks remaining. Serve immediately.

Selecting Ripe Avocados

The best avocados feel heavy for their size and have unblemished skins that are a uniformly dark color. When you gently press the top of the avocado near the stem, the flesh should feel tender, but the body of the avocado should feel firm but not hard. Once they're ripe, you can stash your avocados in the refrigerator up to 2 days to slow further ripening.

CHIPOTLE GUACAMOLE

CHIPOTLE QUESO BLANCO

Typically Served With: Tortilla Chips

Fans of Chipotle are also fans of Tex-Mex-style queso dip. They asked the chain for years to add it to the menu, and in 2017, Chipotle released their first attempt. Because they used all-natural ingredients, a selling point for all their food, the queso had a bit of a grainy texture, and the flavor was very mild. Fans were not impressed, so Chipotle went back to the drawing board, and in 2020 they introduced their new and improved queso that was creamy and flavorful, and it was a hit! Queso Blanco was rolled out to all Chipotle locations and is available as a side or as an addition to a burrito or bowl.

SERVES 6

1 tablespoon unsalted butter
1/4 cup finely chopped yellow onion
1/2 medium jalapeño, minced
1/2 clove garlic, peeled and minced
2 tablespoons drained canned diced green chilies
1 tablespoon chopped chipotle pepper in adobo
1 cup whole milk
1/2 cup heavy whipping cream
1 teaspoon cornstarch
1 cup shredded deli white American cheese
1/2 cup shredded white Cheddar cheese
1/2 cup shredded Monterey jack cheese

1. In a 2-quart saucepan over medium heat, add butter. Once butter is melted and foaming, add onion and jalapeño. Sauté, stirring often, 2 minutes, then add garlic, green chilies, and chipotle in adobo and cook 30 seconds.
2. Stir in milk, then reduce heat to medium-low.
3. In a small bowl, whisk together cream and cornstarch until smooth and then whisk into milk mixture. Increase heat to medium and cook, stirring constantly, until mixture comes to a simmer, about 5 minutes.
4. Reduce heat to low and whisk in cheeses. Once sauce is smooth, remove from heat and serve immediately.

HOOTERS BUFFALO CHICKEN DIP

Typically Served With: Tortilla Chips

Holidays, game days, birthdays, or gatherings with good food and good friends are a good time for a warm and hearty dip! This dip takes all the best flavors of a trip to Hooters—buffalo sauce, ranch dressing, and chicken—and transforms them into bubbling hot and cheesy dip. Hooters introduced this dip in 2014 for a March Madness basketball promotion and will bring it back occasionally as a limited-time-only menu item. It's rough for fans of this dip to have to wait for news of its return, but with this recipe you can enjoy it anytime the craving strikes!

SERVES 8

8 ounces cream cheese, at room temperature
8 ounces shredded sharp Cheddar cheese
1/2 cup buffalo wing sauce, such as Frank's RedHot
1/2 cup mayonnaise
1/4 cup low-fat buttermilk
1/2 teaspoon onion powder
1/4 teaspoon dried dill
1/4 teaspoon ground black pepper
1/4 teaspoon garlic powder
1/4 teaspoon sea salt
2 cups shredded boneless, skinless rotisserie chicken breast

1. Preheat oven to 350°F and spray an 8" × 8" baking dish with nonstick cooking spray.
2. In a medium bowl, combine cream cheese and Cheddar cheese. Beat with a hand mixer on medium speed until mixture is well combined. Add remaining ingredients and beat on low speed until fully combined.
3. Transfer mixture to prepared pan and bake 20–30 minutes until sides of dip are bubbling and top is lightly browned. Cool 5 minutes before serving.

JASON'S DELI CREAMY FRUIT DIP

Typically Served With: Fresh Fruit

Jason's Deli was founded in 1976 in Beaumont, Texas, by Joe Tortorice Jr., Rusty Coco, Pete Verde, and Pat Broussard. In 1988, Jason's Deli began franchising, and today they have over two hundred locations across the United States. Known for their sandwiches, salad bar, giant baked potatoes, and an array of soups, another popular item on the menu is a creamy dip served with cups of fresh fruit. The recipe for this dip contains a tablespoon of orange syrup, but if you can't find it, you can use the recipe in the sidebar or swap it for 1/4 teaspoon orange extract and 2 teaspoons water.

YIELDS 1 1/2 CUPS, 1/4 CUP PER SERVING

1 cup sour cream
1/2 cup packed light brown sugar
1 tablespoon orange syrup

Combine all ingredients in a blender and purée until smooth, about 1 minute. Transfer to an airtight container and refrigerate 4 hours before serving. Store up to 4 days in the refrigerator.

Orange Syrup

Orange syrup is delicious in iced and hot tea or mixed into sweet dips. To make it at home, combine 1 cup sugar, 1 cup water, 1/2 cup orange juice, and three 1-inch strips of orange zest in a 2-quart saucepan. Heat over medium heat until sugar melts, then remove from heat and let stand until cool, about an hour. Refrigerate up to 2 weeks.

JASON'S DELI CREAMY FRUIT DIP

THE MELTING POT COQ AU VIN FONDUE

Typically Served With: Meat and Vegetables

Originating from Switzerland as a communal meal designed to use up food scraps, fondue grew to popularity in the United States in the 1960s and 1970s as a novel dining concept. Jumping on this dining trend, The Melting Pot opened in 1975 in Maitland, Florida—a suburb of Orlando—and today the chain has over ninety locations. The original menu was limited to three items: Swiss cheese fondue, beef fondue, and chocolate fondue. Today, the menu is still simple but includes more variety, such as this French-inspired Coq Au Vin Fondue that gets its name from the red wine in the cooking broth.

SERVES 6

4 cups chicken stock
2/3 cup red Burgundy wine
1/4 cup finely chopped button mushrooms
1/4 cup finely chopped green onion, green parts only
1/4 cup finely chopped carrot
1 clove garlic, peeled and minced

In a 2-quart saucepan, combine all ingredients and mix well. Heat over medium heat until mixture comes to a boil. Let boil 3 minutes, then either reduce heat to low and serve or transfer to a prepared fondue pot. Serve immediately.

Rolling Out Updates

The Melting Pot is rolling out updates to their restaurants that include new menus and decor. Some locations have not seen any updates since the 1980s, so the renovations are being well received! The new menus arrive after the remodel, so it's a good idea to check before heading over if you want to try the new items.

THE MELTING POT ORIGINAL CHOCOLATE FONDUE

Typically Served With: Cake and Fruit

Attention, chocolate lovers! This is the classic dessert fondue that fans have been craving for nearly 50 years! The secret to keeping this fondue smooth and creamy is to maintain a low heat—the chocolate can break up if it gets too hot—and to mix in the chocolate off the heat. Once all is melted and mixed, transfer to a fondue pot on warm, or you can serve the fondue in the cooking pot wrapped in a towel to keep it warm. It probably won't take long to devour, but if it gets too thick, you can rewarm it over low heat until it loosens up.

SERVES 6

1 cup heavy whipping cream
4 ounces milk chocolate chips
2 ounces semisweet chocolate chips
¼ cup crunchy peanut butter

1. In a 1-quart saucepan over medium heat, add cream. Heat, stirring often, until edges of cream start to bubble.
2. Remove pot from heat and add chocolate chips and peanut butter. Let stand 2 minutes, then stir until chocolate is melted and peanut butter is well mixed. Serve immediately.

Fondue Dinner Experience!

The Melting Pot is known for their Four-Course Dinner for Two that includes your choice of cheese fondue, a fresh salad, your choice of an entrée protein with your favorite fondue broth or oil for cooking and dipping sauces to customize your experience, and a chocolate fondue for dessert.

THE MELTING POT ORIGINAL CHOCOLATE FONDUE

THE MELTING POT SPINACH ARTICHOKE FONDUE

Typically Served With: Bread, Fruit, and Vegetables

This marriage of spinach and artichoke dip and fondue is heavenly! With chunks of crusty bread or crisp vegetables for dipping, this makes an excellent appetizer, party dip, or dinner for lovers of creamy, cheesy comfort. To keep the cheese from splitting while melting, a little cornstarch is added. This helps stabilize the emulsion of broth and cheese but does not impact flavor or make things too thick. Rubbing the garlic clove inside the pot gives this fondue a mild garlic flavor, but if you would enjoy more garlic flavor, chop up the ½ clove and add it with the spinach at the start of cooking.

SERVES 6

½ clove garlic, peeled
½ cup Chablis wine
1 cup loosely chopped baby spinach
½ cup canned artichoke hearts in brine, drained, rinsed, and chopped
8 ounces Butterkäse cheese, grated
2 ounces Fontina cheese, grated
2 ounces Parmesan cheese, grated
1 teaspoon cornstarch

1. Wipe the inside of a 1-quart saucepan with garlic clove. Discard clove.
2. Place saucepan over medium heat and add wine, spinach, and artichoke hearts. Whisk to combine, then cook, stirring constantly, until mixture starts to simmer, about 6 minutes.
3. While wine mixture heats, in a medium bowl add cheeses and cornstarch and toss to combine, coating cheeses in cornstarch.
4. Reduce heat to low and slowly whisk in cheeses, a large pinch at a time, until all cheese is melted and smooth.
5. Transfer to a heated fondue pot or serve directly from cooking pot. Serve immediately.

Butterkäse

Butterkäse is a semisoft German cheese that gets its name from its buttery flavor and smooth, soft texture. The flavor is mild, and the cheese delicious on sandwiches, in sauces, or in fondue. If you are unable to find it, Gouda or Muenster are good replacements.

THE MELTING POT WISCONSIN CHEDDAR FONDUE

Typically Served With: Bread, Fruit, and Vegetables

The Melting Pot started with three different fondue recipes, and this is one of them! The Wisconsin Cheddar Fondue starts with domestic beer, adds some spices, and then whisks in a blend of Wisconsin sharp Cheddar cheese and nutty Emmentaler cheese. In the restaurant, they prepare their fondues over a double boiler, which consists of two saucepans, one on top of the other. You can use a double boiler at home if you like, but it is just as easy to make this fondue in a regular saucepan and transfer it to your home fondue set or enjoy it directly from the pan!

SERVES 4

1/2 cup Samuel Adams Boston Lager
1 clove garlic, peeled and minced
1 teaspoon Worcestershire sauce
1/2 teaspoon dry mustard powder
6 ounces sharp Cheddar cheese, grated
4 ounces Emmentaler cheese, grated
1 teaspoon cornstarch

1. Place saucepan over medium heat and add beer, garlic, Worcestershire sauce, and mustard powder. Whisk to combine, then cook, stirring constantly, until mixture starts to simmer, about 6 minutes.
2. While beer mixture heats, in a medium bowl add cheeses and cornstarch and toss to combine, coating cheeses in cornstarch.
3. Once beer mixture is heated, reduce heat to low and slowly whisk in cheeses, a large pinch at a time, until all cheese is melted and smooth.
4. Transfer to a heated fondue pot or serve directly from cooking pot. Serve immediately.

Fixing Lumpy Fondue

Cheese can be a bit tricky to work with, and when mixing into liquids it will sometimes seize, leaving stringy clumps of cheese in your fondue. One easy way to fix a fondue that is looking lumpy is to add a few drops of lemon juice. The acid helps relax the proteins in the cheese!

ON THE BORDER MEXICAN GRILL & CANTINA SIGNATURE QUESO

Typically Served With: Tortilla Chips

At On The Border, they serve a traditional Tex-Mex-style queso made with vegetables and cheese, but have you ever wondered where "queso" comes from? "Queso" is short for "chili con queso," a blend of melted cheese and chilies usually served with tortilla chips for dipping. Prevailing theories about chili con queso are that it is a form of queso flameado from the state of Chihuahua in Mexico. This dish consists of hot melted cheese served with a chorizo topping. Between 1900 and 1920, recipes for Tex-Mex-style queso started to appear in newspapers and cookbooks across California, the Southwest, and Texas, and it quickly became a popular dish.

SERVES 6

1 tablespoon unsalted butter
1/4 cup chopped yellow onion
1/4 cup chopped poblano pepper
1/4 teaspoon onion powder
1/4 teaspoon garlic powder
1 cup whole milk
1/2 cup half-and-half
1 cup shredded deli American cheese
1/2 cup shredded Monterey jack cheese
1/4 cup shredded sharp Cheddar cheese
1/4 cup diced Roma tomato
1 tablespoon finely chopped cilantro leaves

1. In a 2-quart saucepan over medium heat, add butter. Once butter is melted and foaming, add onion, poblano pepper, onion powder, and garlic powder. Sauté until onion and pepper are tender, about 3 minutes.
2. Stir in milk and half-and-half. Reduce heat to medium-low heat and cook, stirring constantly, until mixture starts to steam, 3–5 minutes. Add half American cheese and whisk until cheese is fully melted, then add remaining American cheese and whisk until smooth, about 3 minutes. Whisk in Monterey jack and Cheddar cheeses until smooth.
3. Stir in tomato and cilantro. Serve immediately.

Why Deli American Cheese?

Deli American cheese is often called for in creamy cheese sauces and dips because of its smooth texture. It is made from different cheeses mixed with milk and other ingredients. All American cheese contains emulsifiers to help keep it smooth. Deli style has a higher fat content and contains more cheese, so it offers a richer flavor.

RUTH'S CHRIS STEAK HOUSE GOAT CHEESE & ARTICHOKE DIP

Typically Served With: Toast

When you dine at Ruth's Chris Steak House, you should come hungry, because aside from the delicious steaks and side dishes, they also offer delicious appetizers! One of the most popular is their Goat Cheese & Artichoke Dip. Fans rave on social media about the tangy dip with the hearty texture. It is loaded with artichoke hearts, spinach, and sun-dried tomatoes, then mixed with some cream cheese and mozzarella and plenty of crumbled goat cheese. All this is baked to a bubbling golden brown! For a darker topping, you can broil the dip at 500°F 1 minute or until top is browned to your liking.

SERVES 6

1 tablespoon unsalted butter
1/4 cup chopped yellow onion
2 cups packed whole baby spinach, chopped
1 clove garlic, peeled and minced
1/4 teaspoon ground black pepper
1 (13.75-ounce) can quartered artichoke hearts in brine, drained, rinsed, and chopped
1/4 cup chopped sun-dried tomatoes
4 ounces cream cheese, at room temperature
1/3 cup shredded mozzarella cheese
8 ounces crumbled goat cheese, divided

1. Preheat oven to 400°F and spray a 6-inch oval baking dish with nonstick cooking spray.
2. In a 10-inch skillet over medium heat, add butter. Once butter is melted and foaming, add onion and sauté 3 minutes. Add spinach and cook until fully wilted, about 3 minutes, then add garlic and pepper and cook until garlic is fragrant, about 1 minute.
3. Transfer spinach mixture to a medium bowl and add artichokes, sun-dried tomatoes, cream cheese, and mozzarella. Mix until cream cheese is smooth and mixture is well combined. Fold in half the goat cheese, then transfer to prepared baking dish and top with remaining goat cheese.
4. Bake 20–25 minutes until dip is bubbling and goat cheese on top is browning. Cool 5 minutes before serving. Serve warm.

TORCHY'S TACOS GREEN CHILE QUESO

Typically Served With: Tortilla Chips

What started as a humble food truck in 2006 in Austin, Texas, has become something of a taco empire with over one hundred locations in fourteen states! Founded by Mike Rypka, Torchy's Tacos started as a place to experiment with flavors, fusing traditional Mexican flavors with American and world cuisine. One of the most popular sides on the menu is their Green Chile Queso consisting of a smooth cheese sauce topped with a scoop of guacamole, hot sauce, cotija cheese, and fresh cilantro. You can make it Hillbilly style by adding a scoop of chorizo on top.

SERVES 6

1 cup whole milk
½ cup half-and-half
1 cup shredded deli American cheese
¼ cup tomato salsa, such as Abuelo's Mexican Restaurant Salsa Especial (Chapter 2)
1 (4-ounce) can diced green chilies, drained
¼ teaspoon garlic powder
½ cup shredded Monterey jack cheese
¼ cup shredded sharp Cheddar cheese
¼ teaspoon fresh lime juice
¼ cup guacamole (such as Chipotle Guacamole in this chapter)
2 tablespoons finely chopped cilantro leaves
2 tablespoons crumbled cotija cheese
1 tablespoon Mexican-style hot sauce, such as Valentina

1. In a 2-quart saucepan over medium heat, add milk and half-and-half. Heat, stirring constantly, until milk and half-and-half are steaming.
2. Reduce heat to low and add half American cheese and whisk until cheese is fully melted, then add remaining American cheese and whisk until smooth, about 3 minutes. Stir in salsa, green chilies, and garlic powder and mix well.
3. Whisk in Monterey jack and Cheddar cheeses, adding a large pinch at a time, until smooth, then whisk in lime juice. Remove from heat.
4. In a serving dish, add guacamole in center. Pour over queso, then garnish with cilantro and cotija cheese and drizzle hot sauce over top. Serve immediately.

CHAPTER 10

DELICIOUS DIPPERS: DIPPABLE SIDES FOR PAIRING WITH SECRET SAUCES

You have all the dips, dressings, marinades, and sauces. Now, let's talk dippers! A good dip needs a good dipper, and homemade dippers are almost always better than store-bought. The recipes in this chapter give you options that work for nearly every dip in this book, and they are easy to make so you can start enjoying your dip and dipper creations as quickly as possible. Looking for the right chip for Chipotle Guacamole or Queso Blanco (Chapter 9)? Make a batch of Chipotle Chips for the full restaurant experience! Craving breakfast? Make a batch of KFC Biscuits and smother them in Bob Evans Sausage Gravy (Chapter 8), or make a batch of light and fluffy IHOP Original Buttermilk Pancakes and enjoy them with Snooze, an A.M. Eatery Vanilla Cream Sauce (Chapter 8). Love fried shrimp? Make Red Lobster's crave-worthy Walt's Favorite Shrimp and pair them with Bubba Gump Shrimp Co. Remoulade Sauce (Chapter 5). Mixing and matching dippers is also fun, so make some Olive Garden Calamari and enjoy it with Jimmy John's Kickin' Ranch (Chapter 4) or Wendy's Creamy Sriracha Sauce (Chapter 2). The options are nearly endless when you have so many delicious dipper options!

BUFFALO WILD WINGS CHEDDAR CHEESE CURDS

Typically Served With: Southwestern Ranch

Crispy fried cheese is never a bad idea! At Buffalo Wild Wings, cheese curds remain one of the most popular appetizers on the menu. They are typically served with your choice of dipping sauce, but they are good with anything from ranch to marinara, or all on their own! A few tips for success: First, put your cheese curds in the freezer for 20 minutes before frying to keep the cheese from melting too quickly. Second, let the batter rest for a few minutes after mixing so the flour has time to relax in order to make a crisper batter. Finally, eat these fresh! They lose their crispy magic when they cool down.

SERVES 4

Vegetable oil, for frying
1¼ cups all-purpose flour, divided
1 teaspoon baking powder
¼ teaspoon sea salt
¼ teaspoon paprika
½ cup low-fat buttermilk
½ cup club soda
16 ounces Cheddar cheese curds, placed in freezer 20 minutes

1. Fill a deep fryer with oil per manufacturer directions and heat to 350°F. Or in a 5½-quart Dutch oven, add enough oil to fill pot by 3 inches, leaving at least 3 inches of space at the top, and place over medium-high heat until oil reaches 350°F.
2. In a medium bowl, combine 1 cup flour, baking powder, salt, and paprika. Whisk to combine, then add buttermilk and club soda and whisk until batter is smooth. Let batter rest 5 minutes.
3. In a large resealable plastic bag, combine remaining flour with cheese curds. Seal bag and shake to evenly coat cheese curds. Remove from bag and tap off excess.
4. Working with 5 or 6 curds at a time, dip curds in batter 1 at a time and immediately add to hot oil. Fry 2 minutes per side or until puffed and golden brown.
5. Transfer cooked curds to a paper towel–lined plate to drain. Repeat with remaining curds. Serve immediately.

What Are Cheese Curds?

A cheese curd is cheese that has separated from the whey but has not been pressed into a larger block or wheel of cheese. Cheese curds have a squeaky feel on the teeth when eaten cold. You can find plain or flavored varieties in bags at most grocery stores.

BUFFALO WILD WINGS FRIED PICKLES

Typically Served With: Southwestern Ranch

In 2011, Buffalo Wild Wings introduced Fried Pickles as a menu item to take advantage of the surge in popularity fried pickles were experiencing at the time. The history of fried pickles traces back to the 1960s, when they were created in Arkansas by the Duchess Drive-In in 1963. Fried pickles were a bit of a niche Southern favorite until the early 2010s, when they went from cult classic snack to nationwide bar food favorite. These reheat well in an air fryer, if you happen to have leftovers. Preheat the air fryer to 375°F and air fry 5–7 minutes until pickles are hot and crisp.

SERVES 6

1 cup all-purpose flour, divided
2 tablespoons cornmeal
2 tablespoons cornstarch
1 teaspoon Cajun seasoning
½ teaspoon paprika
½ teaspoon cayenne pepper
¼ teaspoon ground black pepper
1 cup club soda, chilled
Vegetable oil, for frying
2 cups thick-cut dill pickle slices, drained and patted dry

1. In a medium bowl, combine ½ cup flour, cornmeal, cornstarch, Cajun seasoning, paprika, cayenne pepper, and black pepper. Whisk well to combine.
2. Slowly whisk in club soda until batter is smooth. Cover and refrigerate batter while you heat oil.
3. Fill a deep fryer with oil per manufacturer directions and heat to 350°F. Or in a 5½-quart Dutch oven, add enough oil to fill pot by 3 inches, leaving at least 3 inches of space at the top, and place over medium-high heat until oil reaches 350°F.
4. In a resealable bag, add remaining flour and pickle slices. Shake to coat pickles. Remove batter from refrigerator and stir well, then dunk pickle slices, 5 or 6 at a time, in batter, then transfer to hot oil. Fry 2–3 minutes until pickles are golden brown. Serve immediately.

Southwestern Ranch

To make a quick dupe for Buffalo Wild Wings Southwestern Ranch, combine 1 cup prepared ranch dressing (Wingstop Ranch in Chapter 3 would be perfect here) with 2 teaspoons taco seasoning, 1 teaspoon chili powder, and ¼ teaspoon smoked paprika. Mix, then chill for 1 hour before serving.

BUFFALO WILD WINGS FRIED PICKLES

CHICK-FIL-A NUGGETS

Typically Served With: Chick-fil-A Sauce

Chick-fil-A Nuggets were added to the chain's menu in 1982 and have been a menu staple ever since! They are as delicious as they are versatile. Add them to a breakfast scramble, toss them onto a salad, fold them into a wrap, or stuff them into mini yeast rolls, just to name a few ways to enjoy them. Of course, you can also eat them as they are with your favorite Chick-fil-A dips, like Honey Mustard, Polynesian, or Chick-fil-A Sauce, all found in Chapter 3 of this book.

SERVES 4

8 ounces chicken breast tenders, cut into 1-inch pieces
1/4 cup low-fat buttermilk
2 tablespoons dill pickle brine
1 teaspoon granulated sugar
Vegetable oil, for frying
1/2 cup all-purpose flour
1 teaspoon ground black pepper
1/2 teaspoon salt
1/2 teaspoon paprika

1. In a gallon resealable plastic bag, add chicken pieces, buttermilk, pickle brine, and sugar. Seal bag, removing as much air as you can, and massage to evenly coat chicken and combine marinade ingredients. Refrigerate at least 2 hours and up to 24 hours.
2. Remove chicken from refrigerator 30 minutes before cooking to warm to room temperature.
3. Fill a deep fryer with oil per manufacturer directions and heat to 350°F. Or in a 5 1/2-quart Dutch oven, add enough oil to fill pot by 3 inches, leaving at least 3 inches of space at the top, and place over medium-high heat until oil reaches 350°F.
4. In a medium bowl, add flour, pepper, salt, and paprika and mix well to combine. Remove chicken from marinade and let excess drip off. Dredge chicken in flour mixture, shaking off excess flour, and gently place in hot oil. Working in batches, fry 3–5 minutes until chicken reaches an internal temperature of 165°F. Remove chicken from oil and let drain on a paper towel-lined plate. Serve immediately.

CHILI'S BIG MOUTH BITES

Typically Served With: Ranch

Sliders are among the most popular bar food items because they are easy and fun to eat for both adults and kids. At Chili's, they miniaturized their famous Big Mouth Burgers into Big Mouth Bites. These are available as an entrée or as a part of their wildly popular Triple Dipper appetizer. As an entrée, the sliders are sold in groups of four with French fries on the side. On the Triple Dipper, you get two sliders and a side of ranch for dipping. You can prepare the meat mixture for these sliders up to a day ahead, along with sautéing the onions and crumbling the bacon. When you are ready, toast the buns, cook the burgers, and you are ready to eat!

SERVES 4

1½ pounds 85/15 ground beef
2 teaspoons sea salt
1 teaspoon ground black pepper
½ teaspoon garlic powder
¼ teaspoon onion powder
12 slider buns, halved
3 tablespoons vegetable oil
1 medium yellow onion, peeled and chopped
3 slices deli American cheese, cut into quarters
1 cup ranch dressing
8 strips smoked bacon, cooked and crumbled

1. In a medium bowl, combine beef, salt, pepper, garlic powder, and onion powder. Mix to combine, then divide meat into 12 even balls. Cover and refrigerate 1 hour.
2. In a dry 10-inch skillet over medium heat, add buns cut side down. Cook until toasted, 3–5 minutes. Remove from skillet and reserve.
3. To same skillet over medium heat, add oil. Once oil is hot, add onion and cook, stirring constantly, until onion is very tender and starting to brown, about 12 minutes. Transfer to a small bowl and reserve.
4. To same skillet over medium heat, add 4 prepared hamburger balls and gently press with a spatula to flatten each into a ½-inch thick patty. Cook 4–5 minutes per side until burgers are browned and cooked to your preference. During last minute of cooking, top each patty with a piece of American cheese to melt. Repeat with remaining burgers.
5. To assemble, spread ½ teaspoon ranch on both halves of burger buns. Add patty to bottom half of each bun and top with sautéed onion and crumbled bacon. Top with other half of bun and serve with remaining ranch on the side for dipping. Serve immediately.

CHILI'S BONELESS WINGS

Typically Served With: Ranch

In 2020, many restaurants were looking for innovative ways to attract customers for delivery meals. One popular solution was to create a ghost kitchen, or a restaurant within a restaurant that specialized in one or two particular items. These virtual kitchens helped preserve jobs and kept many restaurant chains afloat during a time of uncertainty around the world. Chili's decided to jump on the virtual restaurant concept with their entry into the market: It's Just Wings. This continues to sell traditional and boneless wings, just like those available on the regular Chili's menu, along with fries and desserts.

SERVES 4

1 cup all-purpose flour
2 tablespoons cornstarch
1/2 teaspoon sea salt
1/2 teaspoon ground black pepper
1/4 teaspoon paprika
1/4 teaspoon onion powder
1 large egg
1 cup low-fat buttermilk
1 pound chicken breast tenders, cut into 1-inch pieces
Vegetable oil, for frying
1/2 cup buffalo wing sauce

1. In a large resealable plastic bag, add flour, cornstarch, salt, pepper, paprika, and onion powder. Close bag and shake well to combine. Set aside.
2. In a medium bowl, add egg and beat well. Add buttermilk and whisk to combine.
3. Add chicken pieces to bag with flour, close, and shake to coat. Remove chicken pieces and place on a plate. Dip in buttermilk mixture and then return to bag and coat in flour. Place on a wire rack to let breading set while oil heats.
4. Fill a deep fryer with oil per manufacturer directions and heat to 350°F. Or in a 5 1/2-quart Dutch oven, add enough oil to fill pot by 3 inches, leaving at least 3 inches of space at the top, and place over medium-high heat until oil reaches 350°F.
5. Add 5 or 6 chicken pieces at a time to hot oil and cook 5–6 minutes, turning halfway through cooking time, until chicken is golden brown and reaches an internal temperature of 165°F.
6. Transfer chicken pieces to a paper towel–lined plate to drain. Repeat process with remaining chicken.
7. Once chicken is fried, add to a large bowl along with wing sauce and toss to coat evenly. Serve immediately.

CHILI'S FRIED MOZZARELLA

Typically Served With: Ranch

If you have spent any time on the food side of social media, you have likely seen people happily stretching gooey mozzarella from their mouth and across a table while filming it all for their followers to enjoy! These super-stretchy mozzarella fan favorites have gone viral for their reel-worthy cheese pull and savory flavor. Added to the Chili's menu as Fried Mozzarella in 2022, it did not take long for these appetizers to become darlings of the food influencer set. They are great with ranch or marinara for dipping, or for an extra kick, you can toss them in Chili's Nashville Hot Sauce (Chapter 2) just before serving.

SERVES 4

1 cup all-purpose flour
½ teaspoon sea salt
½ teaspoon ground black pepper
2 large eggs, beaten
½ teaspoon hot pepper sauce
¾ cup fine bread crumbs
1 teaspoon paprika
½ teaspoon onion powder
¼ teaspoon garlic powder
1 (6-ounce) block whole milk mozzarella cheese, cut into ½-inch thick and 3-inch long blocks
Vegetable oil, for frying

1. In a shallow dish, add flour, salt, and pepper. Whisk to combine.
2. In a medium bowl, add eggs and hot sauce. Whisk until fully combined.
3. In a second shallow dish, combine bread crumbs, paprika, onion powder, and garlic powder. Mix well to combine.
4. Roll mozzarella blocks in flour, dip in egg, then return to flour and coat well. Dip again in egg, letting excess drip off, then coat evenly in bread crumbs, pressing to ensure an even coating. Repeat with remaining mozzarella, then transfer to a small parchment-lined baking sheet and freeze 15 minutes.
5. Fill a deep fryer with oil per manufacturer directions and heat to 350°F. Or in a 5½-quart Dutch oven, add enough oil to fill pot by 3 inches, leaving at least 3 inches of space at the top, and place over medium-high heat until oil reaches 350°F.
6. Working in batches, fry mozzarella blocks 2–3 minutes until golden brown and crisp. Transfer to a paper towel–lined plate to cool 2 minutes. Serve immediately.

CHILI'S SOUTHWESTERN EGGROLLS

Typically Served With: Avocado-Ranch

The 1980s were a notable era for fusion cuisine. With Americans being exposed to more international cuisines, restaurants began to play with those flavors, creating new and exciting dishes. One such fusion dish was the Southwestern Eggroll. Shaped and filled like an eggroll but made with Southwestern ingredients, these flavor-packed appetizers quickly became a popular addition to bar and casual dining menus and remain popular today. At Chili's, the Southwestern Eggrolls are packed with beans, vegetables, and cheese and are a delicious vegetarian option. If you want, you can add ⅓ cup shredded cooked chicken breast to amp up the protein.

SERVES 8

1 cup canned black beans, rinsed and drained
1 cup canned whole kernel corn, rinsed and drained
1 cup roughly chopped baby spinach
¼ cup drained pimentos
1 medium jalapeño, chopped
2 cloves garlic, peeled and minced
¼ cup minced yellow onion
½ teaspoon chili powder
½ teaspoon salt
¼ teaspoon ground black pepper
2 cups grated Monterey jack cheese
8 (8-inch) flour tortillas
½ cup vegetable oil

1. In a large mixing bowl, combine beans, corn, spinach, pimentos, jalapeño, garlic, onion, chili powder, salt, pepper, and cheese. Mix well.
2. Place 2 tablespoons mixture on each tortilla and roll into an eggroll shape.
3. Heat a 10-inch skillet over medium-high heat. Working in batches, using 1 tablespoon oil per 2 or 3 eggrolls, shallow fry eggrolls in pan until golden brown, then transfer to a paper towel–lined plate to drain.
4. To serve, slice eggrolls in half diagonally. Serve immediately.

Avocado-Ranch

Add 1 cup prepared ranch dressing (like Wingstop Ranch in Chapter 3) to a blender with half a large ripe avocado. Blend until smooth, about 30 seconds, then stir in ½ teaspoon fresh lime juice. Transfer to an airtight container and refrigerate at least 4 hours before serving.

CHILI'S SOUTHWESTERN EGGROLLS

CHIPOTLE CHIPS

Typically Served With: Guacamole

TikTok has become a treasure trove of restaurants sharing information, and Chipotle is no different. In 2020, Chipotle took to TikTok and shared some of their secrets, and among them was a reel showing fans how they make their popular tortilla chips. These chips are popular for their freshness—they are made in-house throughout the day—and for their unique flavor. They are seasoned not just with salt but with a hint of lime too. Thanks to TikTok, fans were able to demystify the process. And with this recipe, you have a foolproof method for crispy, salty, lime-flavored chips anytime! Pair with Chipotle Guacamole (Chapter 9) for the real restaurant experience.

SERVES 10

Vegetable oil, for frying
20 (5-inch) corn tortillas, cut into quarters
1 large lime, cut in half
1 tablespoon sea salt

1. Fill a deep fryer with oil per manufacturer directions and heat to 350°F. Or in a 5½-quart Dutch oven, add enough oil to fill pot by 3 inches, leaving at least 3 inches of space at the top, and place over medium-high heat until oil reaches 350°F.
2. Fry tortilla wedges in batches, making sure not to overcrowd pot, until crisp and golden brown, 2–3 minutes, flipping over about halfway through cooking.
3. Transfer chips to a baking sheet lined with paper towels. Place half of lime in a citrus juicer and immediately sprinkle chips with lime juice, then sprinkle with salt. Repeat with remaining tortillas, lime juice, and salt. Enjoy immediately or let chips cool to room temperature and store in an airtight plastic container up to 3 days.

Filtering Frying Oil

Frying oil can be used two to three times before it should be discarded as long as it has not been heated over 350°F. Here is how to reuse it: Pour cooled frying oil through a coffee filter-lined strainer into a clean container. Store in a cool, dark place, but if the oil has an off odor or is very dark in color, discard it.

CULVER'S PRETZEL BITES

Typically Served With: Culver's Wisconsin Cheddar Cheese Sauce

The best things often start as limited-time-only menu items! At Culver's, fans waited for the chain to announce the return of their soft, buttery Pretzel Bites. Fans begged and pleaded, and in 2021, their pleas were answered when Culver's announced the Pretzel Bites were not only returning, they were going to be a permanent addition to the menu. Said Director of Menu Development Quinn Adkins, "We heard our guests loud and clear, and we added these to our menu permanently on April 5, 2021." Pair them with your favorite dips like yellow mustard or Culver's Wisconsin Cheddar Cheese Sauce (Chapter 7).

SERVES 4

1¾ cups warm water, divided
½ teaspoons active dry yeast
1 tablespoon packed light brown sugar
½ teaspoons sea salt
½ cup bread flour
1½ cups all-purpose flour
2 tablespoons baking soda
1½ tablespoons pretzel salt
4 tablespoons melted salted butter

1. Add ¾ cup water to a medium mixing bowl and add yeast. Stir to dissolve. Let stand 5 minutes.
2. To yeast mixture, add brown sugar and salt. Stir to dissolve. Add flours and knead dough by hand until smooth and elastic, about 12 minutes.
3. Let dough rise on the countertop at least 30 minutes or until doubled in bulk.
4. While dough is rising, combine remaining water and baking soda in a medium bowl. Stir often.
5. Preheat oven to 400°F and line a half baking sheet with baking parchment sprayed lightly with nonstick cooking spray.
6. After dough has risen, divide into 24 pieces. Dip each piece in baking soda solution and then place on prepared baking sheet. Sprinkle with pretzel salt.
7. Bake 10–12 minutes until golden. Brush with melted butter and serve.

IHOP ORIGINAL BUTTERMILK PANCAKES

Typically Served With: Pancake Syrup

Fluffy, melt-in-your-mouth pancakes are a thing of beauty, and IHOP understands this better than most! Their Original Buttermilk Pancakes are the flagship recipe for the chain and one of the things that keeps fans coming back again and again. In one viral TikTok video, a fan was so eager for her pancakes as the server was delivering them, she did a happy dance in her booth, much to the distraction of at least one other diner. These pancakes are the perfect canvas for toppings and can be dressed up or kept simple. You can make them ahead and reheat them in a microwave 20–30 seconds on high before eating.

YIELDS 8, 2 PANCAKES PER SERVING

1⅓ cups all-purpose flour
1 teaspoon baking powder
1 teaspoon baking soda
½ teaspoon salt
1⅓ cups low-fat buttermilk
1 large egg
¼ cup vegetable oil
¼ cup granulated sugar

1. In a medium bowl, combine flour, baking powder, baking soda, and salt. Whisk to combine.
2. In a separate medium bowl, combine buttermilk, egg, oil, and sugar and whisk until smooth.
3. Add wet ingredients to dry ingredients and mix with a spatula until just combined and no large clumps of flour remain, about 20 strokes.
4. Preheat a two-burner griddle over medium heat and spray with nonstick cooking spray.
5. Add two ⅓-cup scoops of batter onto hot griddle and cook 2–4 minutes per side until browned. Transfer to a plate and cover with a clean towel to keep warm while you cook remaining batter. Serve warm.

Picture-Perfect Pancake Secrets

Want the perfect, smooth, Instagram-ready pancakes every time? Try this trick. Instead of using nonstick cooking spray, dab a paper towel in vegetable oil and wipe your griddle with it until a very fine film remains. Cook pancakes as directed, wiping the griddle with the paper towel between pancakes.

KFC BISCUITS

Typically Served With: Original Recipe Chicken

KFC did not always offer biscuits on their menu. Instead, they offered dinner rolls with their chicken. Sometime in the early 1980s, KFC made the switch and has not looked back! The biscuits have a bit of a cakey texture and are made with milk, not buttermilk, so they are savory but not tangy. These can be served as a side with butter and honey. Or you can split them and serve them for breakfast with Bob Evans Sausage Gravy (Chapter 8), or make a sandwich with chicken tenders or fried egg, bacon, and cheese.

YIELDS 8, 2 BISCUITS PER SERVING

2 cups all-purpose flour
1 tablespoon baking powder
1 tablespoon granulated sugar
½ teaspoon cream of tartar
½ teaspoon sea salt
½ cup salted butter, cubed and chilled
⅔ cup whole milk, chilled

1. Preheat oven to 400°F and line a half baking sheet with parchment.
2. In a large bowl, mix together flour, baking powder, sugar, cream of tartar, and salt. With your fingers, rub butter in flour until butter is fully combined and mixture resembles coarse sand. Cover and chill mixture 10 minutes.
3. Make a well in dry ingredients and add milk. Gently stir until dough forms a shaggy ball. Turn dough out onto a lightly floured surface and press into a ½-inch-thick rectangle, then fold dough in half. You may need to use a spatula or bench scraper for the first few times, as dough will be shaggy. Turn the dough a quarter turn and repeat this process four more times. Cover dough and chill 10 minutes.
4. Once dough is chilled, use your hands to form dough into an 8" × 10" rectangle approximately ½ inch thick. Use a 3-inch biscuit cutter and cut biscuits by pressing straight down and lifting straight up. This will help your layers stay separate. Transfer biscuits to prepared baking sheet, placing biscuits with sides just touching. Gather scraps, re-form into a rectangle, and cut remaining biscuits.
5. Bake 15–20 minutes until biscuits are puffed and golden brown. Cool on the pan 5 minutes before enjoying.

Sugar Scrap Biscuits

Press remaining scraps of dough into 2-inch rounds, and without bothering to roll or flatten the dough, bake as directed in recipe. Brush them with melted butter and sprinkle with sugar before eating. They won't be pretty, but this is delicious and a fun way to avoid food waste!

LONGHORN STEAKHOUSE TEXAS TONION

Typically Served With: Zesty Dip

Battered and deep-fried onions, be they onion rings, petals, or a blooming flower, are a popular appetizer at most steakhouses. At LongHorn Steakhouse, they serve a tempting "Texas-sized" appetizer of battered and fried onion petals perfect for snacking on while awaiting an entrée. Cutting onions into petals makes them easier to eat than the blooming-style appetizer, and a pile of crispy fried onions is simply fun to enjoy! This appetizer is absolutely begging for a side of Outback Steakhouse Bloomin' Onion Sauce (Chapter 7) or some Raising Cane's Cane's Sauce (Chapter 3).

SERVES 4

1 large Vidalia or Texas sweet onion
Vegetable oil, for frying
1¼ cups all-purpose flour, divided
1 teaspoon garlic powder, divided
1 teaspoon paprika, divided
½ teaspoon sea salt, divided
½ teaspoon ground black pepper, divided
¼ teaspoon cayenne pepper, divided
3 tablespoons cornstarch
12 ounces lager beer

1. Cut about ¾ inch off top of onion and peel. Cut 12 vertical wedges, then cut off root end and separate wedges into onion petals. Set aside.
2. Fill a deep fryer with oil per manufacturer directions and heat to 350°F. Or in a 5½-quart Dutch oven, add enough oil to fill pot by 3 inches, leaving at least 3 inches of space at the top, and place over medium-high heat until oil reaches 350°F.
3. In a medium bowl, whisk together 1 cup flour, ½ teaspoon garlic powder, ½ teaspoon paprika, ¼ teaspoon salt, ¼ teaspoon black pepper, and ⅛ teaspoon cayenne pepper. Set aside.
4. In a separate medium bowl, combine remaining flour, remaining spices, cornstarch, and beer and whisk until mixture forms a smooth batter.
5. Add onion petals to seasoned flour mixture. Dip in batter, then return to flour. Transfer to hot oil, making sure not to overcrowd pot, and fry 3–5 minutes until onion petals are golden brown and crisp. You may need to work in batches. Transfer to a paper towel–lined plate to drain. Serve immediately.

OLIVE GARDEN BREADSTICKS

Typically Served With: Alfredo Sauce

When you think of Olive Garden, one of the first things that likely comes to mind are their warm breadsticks. Servers bring out a basket with one breadstick per person, and if you like more, they will bring out additional baskets with one breadstick per person. Yes, they are unlimited, so guests can indulge in as many as they like, but Olive Garden also wants to prevent food waste by limiting the number of breadsticks per basket delivered. You can also enjoy the full restaurant experience by serving a cup of warm Olive Garden Marinara or Alfredo Sauce (both in Chapter 8) as a dip for your breadsticks!

SERVES 6

1 (10.5-ounce/6 count) package frozen breadsticks
2 tablespoons unsalted butter, melted
¼ cup Parmesan cheese

1. Preheat oven to 350°F.
2. Brush each breadstick with butter. Sprinkle the top of each breadstick with Parmesan cheese and wrap breadsticks in aluminum foil.
3. Bake directly on oven rack 12–15 minutes until breadsticks are hot. Unwrap and serve immediately.

Pasta Passes

In 2018, Olive Garden offered a limited number of annual pasta passes to fans for $300. One thousand lucky fans were able to purchase the pass, which entitled them to 52 weeks of unlimited pasta. Current passes include the Never-Ending Pasta Pass (subject to availability), offering 9 weeks of delicious soup, salad, breadsticks, and pasta, and a $500 Lifetime Pasta Pass.

OLIVE GARDEN CALAMARI

Typically Served With: Marinara Sauce and Spicy Ranch

Fried calamari is a staple of Italian restaurant appetizer menus because of its connection to coastal Italian cuisine. At Olive Garden, it comes out hot, crisp, and very tender accompanied by cups of Spicy Ranch and Marinara Sauce (Chapter 8) for dipping! The secret to tender calamari is to not overcook it. You want to remove it from the hot oil as soon as the breading has started to turn golden brown, 2–3 minutes. You will also want to thoroughly dry the calamari rings before breading so the breading adheres properly and does not slide off while frying.

SERVES 4

Vegetable oil, for frying
1 cup all-purpose flour
1/2 teaspoon Italian seasoning
1/2 teaspoon garlic powder
1/2 teaspoon onion powder
1/2 teaspoon sea salt
1/2 teaspoon ground black pepper
1/4 teaspoon baking powder
1 pound frozen calamari rings, drained and patted dry
1/2 cup low-fat buttermilk
1/2 teaspoon dried parsley
2 lemon wedges

1. Fill a deep fryer with oil per manufacturer directions and heat to 350°F. Or in a 5 1/2-quart Dutch oven, add enough oil to fill pot by 3 inches, leaving at least 3 inches of space at the top, and place over medium-high heat until oil reaches 350°F.
2. In a medium bowl, combine flour, Italian seasoning, garlic powder, onion powder, salt, pepper, and baking powder. Whisk to mix thoroughly.
3. Add calamari rings to seasoned flour. Toss to coat evenly. Pour buttermilk in a separate medium bowl and dip rings in buttermilk, then return to flour and coat rings again.
4. Transfer rings to hot oil, making sure not to overcrowd pot, and fry 2–3 minutes until rings are golden brown and crisp. You may need to work in batches. Transfer to a paper towel–lined plate to drain. Garnish with parsley and lemon wedges. Serve immediately.

OLIVE GARDEN TOASTED RAVIOLI

Typically Served With: Marinara Sauce

The prevailing theory goes that in the 1940s in St. Louis, Missouri, a chef in the Hill neighborhood accidentally dropped a ravioli into a deep fryer and was so impressed with the result that the dish was added to the menu. The exact restaurant and chef remain murky since there are multiple claims for the dish's creation, but what we do know is that these ravioli are delicious and a fun appetizer, snack, or party finger food. At Olive Garden, Toasted Ravioli has been on the menu for years and remains a popular appetizer with fans. You will find it served with Marinara Sauce (Chapter 8), but it is also great with ranch or Alfredo Sauce (Chapter 8).

SERVES 4

1/4 cup water
2 large eggs
1 teaspoon Italian seasoning
1/2 teaspoon garlic powder
1/2 teaspoon sea salt
1 cup plain bread crumbs
1 cup all-purpose flour
Vegetable oil, for frying
1 (16-ounce) package meat-filled ravioli
1 tablespoon freshly grated Parmesan cheese
1 teaspoon dried parsley

1. In a small bowl, mix water and eggs and beat well. Set aside.
2. In a separate small bowl, mix Italian seasoning, garlic powder, and salt with bread crumbs and set aside.
3. In a third small bowl, add flour and set aside.
4. Fill a deep fryer with oil per manufacturer directions and heat to 350°F. Or in a 5 1/2-quart Dutch oven, add enough oil to fill pot by 3 inches, leaving at least 3 inches of space at the top, and place over medium-high heat until oil reaches 350°F.
5. Dip ravioli in flour, then in eggs, then in bread crumbs and carefully place in hot oil.
6. Fry ravioli in batches of 3 or 4, 2–3 minutes until golden; remove from oil; and drain on a paper towel–lined plate. Garnish ravioli with Parmesan and parsley. Serve warm.

OUTBACK STEAKHOUSE GOLD COAST COCONUT SHRIMP

Typically Served With: Creole Marmalade

In the 1960s and 1970s, riding the wave of the addition of Hawaii as the fiftieth US state, coconut shrimp exploded in popularity along with tiki culture. Restaurants, never shy to jump on a popular trend, began adding coconut shrimp to their menus to add an exotic flair. Over time, the exotic nature of the dish faded away, and now it is a classic appetizer and party food. Outback Steakhouse has had Gold Coast Coconut Shrimp on the menu for many years, and they pair it with Creole Marmalade (Chapter 7) for a sweet and zesty kick.

SERVES 4

2 (7-ounce) bags shredded coconut, divided
1/4 cup granulated sugar
1 teaspoon sea salt
1 1/2 cups all-purpose flour
1 1/2 cups lager beer
Vegetable oil, for frying
24 tail-on peeled and deveined jumbo shrimp

1. In a medium bowl, combine 1 cup coconut, sugar, salt, flour, and beer. Mix well, cover, and refrigerate at least 1 hour.
2. Fill a deep fryer with oil per manufacturer directions and heat to 350°F. Or in a 5 1/2-quart Dutch oven, add enough oil to fill pot by 3 inches, leaving at least 3 inches of space at the top, and place over medium-high heat until oil reaches 350°F.
3. Pour remaining coconut in a shallow bowl. Dip 1 shrimp at a time in batter, then roll battered shrimp in coconut.
4. Fry shrimp a few at a time in hot oil until golden brown, 2–3 minutes. Drain on a paper towel–lined plate. Repeat with remaining shrimp and batter. Serve immediately.

Tiki Culture

Americans' interest in tiki culture goes back to the 1930s. The first tiki bar is thought to have been Don's Beachcomber in Hollywood, California, which was opened in 1933 by Ernest Raymond Beaumont Gantt, a former rum runner from Texas and Louisiana. In 1937, the bar moved across the street and expanded into a restaurant called Don the Beachcomber. The restaurant served rum cocktails, tropical drinks, and Chinese food.

P.F. CHANG'S PORK DUMPLINGS

Typically Served With: Savory Chili Sauce

It is believed that pot stickers—dumplings that are allowed to crisp on the bottom before being steamed—are a happy accident born of a chef of the Chinese imperial court accidentally leaving dumplings on a hot stove until the bottoms browned. Rather than discard the dumplings, this chef decided to go ahead and steam them. The result was both crisp and tender with a juicy filling. P.F. Chang's offers these dumplings on their appetizer menu along with a side of spicy dipping sauce, like Din Tai Fung House Spicy Sauce (Chapter 8).

SERVES 4

1 pound ground pork
1/2 cup finely shredded napa cabbage
1/4 cup chopped green onion, green parts only
1 tablespoon soy sauce
1 teaspoon rice vinegar
1 teaspoon sesame oil
1/2 teaspoon freshly grated ginger
1/2 teaspoon granulated sugar
24 dumpling wrappers
1/2 cup plus 2 tablespoons water, divided
2 tablespoons vegetable oil, divided

1. In a medium bowl, combine pork, cabbage, green onion, soy sauce, rice vinegar, sesame oil, ginger, and sugar. Mix until fully combined, then cover and refrigerate 1 hour.
2. To prepare dumplings, lay a wrapper on a work surface. Spoon 1 teaspoon filling onto center of wrapper. Dip finger in 2 tablespoons water and run along edge of wrapper. Fold wrapper and pleat sides. Repeat with remaining filling and wrappers.
3. Heat a 10-inch nonstick skillet with a lid over medium heat. Add 1 tablespoon oil and swirl to coat bottom of skillet evenly. Add 10 dumplings to skillet and let cook, not moving, 3–4 minutes until bottoms of dumplings are deeply golden brown.
4. Add 1/4 cup water to skillet, cover with lid, and let steam 8–10 minutes until filling is cooked through, wrappers are tender, and filling reaches an internal temperature of 165°F. Repeat with remaining dumplings, oil, and water. Serve immediately.

Steaming Instructions

To steam dumplings, place a large pot on the stove filled by a few inches with water. Top pot with a steamer basket that has a lid. Line steamer basket with one layer of napa cabbage leaves. Lay dumplings on leaves, making sure they do not touch, and steam 10–15 minutes or until filling reaches an internal temperature of 165°F. You may need to work in batches.

RAISING CANE'S CHICKEN FINGERS

Typically Served With: Cane's Sauce

It may not be possible for a combination to be more viral than Raising Cane's Chicken Fingers with a big cup of Cane's Sauce! This dynamic duo began to gain social media popularity in 2018, with more than one social media food enthusiast going viral. It is uncommon to find American mukbang content creators out there who have not shared at least one Raising Cane's related video with their fans. If you prefer, you can cut whole boneless, skinless chicken breasts into 1-inch strips and use these in place of chicken tenders and cook as directed here.

SERVES 4

1 cup low-fat buttermilk
1 large egg, beaten
1 tablespoon sea salt, divided
1 tablespoon paprika, divided
2 teaspoons garlic powder, divided
2 teaspoons onion powder, divided
16 chicken tenders
1 cup all-purpose flour
1/4 cup cornstarch
1/2 teaspoon baking powder
1/2 teaspoon ground black pepper
Vegetable oil, for frying

1. In a medium bowl with a lid, add buttermilk, egg, and 1 teaspoon each salt, paprika, garlic powder, and onion powder. Whisk well to combine. Add tenders and stir to mix, making sure tenders are evenly coated. Cover and refrigerate 2 hours up to overnight. Remove chicken from refrigerator 1 hour before you plan to start cooking.
2. In a resealable plastic bag, combine remaining spices, flour, cornstarch, baking powder, and pepper. Reseal and shake well to mix.
3. Remove tenders from buttermilk mixture 2 or 3 at a time, add to bag, seal, and shake to coat with flour. Transfer to a half baking sheet with a wire rack on top. Repeat with remaining tenders.
4. Fill a deep fryer with oil per manufacturer directions and heat to 350°F. Or in a 5 1/2-quart Dutch oven, add enough oil to fill pot by 3 inches, leaving at least 3 inches of space at the top, and place over medium-high heat until oil reaches 350°F.
5. Add tenders 3 or 4 at a time to hot oil. Cook, turning often, until tenders are golden brown and reach an internal temperature of 165°F, 7–10 minutes. Let tenders drain on a paper-towel lined plate. Repeat with remaining tenders. Serve immediately.

RED LOBSTER WALT'S FAVORITE SHRIMP

Typically Served With: Cocktail Sauce

In recent years, Red Lobster has become known as the place for shrimp. Be it their discontinued endless shrimp promotion or their Shrimp Your Way meals, Red Lobster fans love their shrimp! In this version, named for longtime employee Walter "Walt" King, the shrimp are breaded and fried until crisp and served with Red Lobster Cocktail Sauce (Chapter 5). Making these at home, you can enjoy them with any sauce you like, so also consider Red Lobster Tartar Sauce or Bubba Gump Shrimp Co. Remoulade Sauce (both in Chapter 5).

SERVES 4

24 tail-on peeled and deveined jumbo shrimp, butterflied
1 cup all-purpose flour
1 teaspoon seafood seasoning, such as Old Bay
½ teaspoon sea salt
¼ teaspoon baking powder
½ cup whole milk
½ cup vegetable oil, plus more for frying
1 large egg, beaten

1. Pat shrimp dry with paper towels. Set aside.
2. In a medium bowl, combine flour, seafood seasoning, salt, and baking powder.
3. In a separate medium bowl, combine milk, ½ cup oil, and egg. Whisk until mixture is smooth.
4. Fill a deep fryer with oil per manufacturer directions and heat to 350°F. Or in a 5½-quart Dutch oven, add enough oil to fill pot by 3 inches, leaving at least 3 inches of space at the top, and place over medium-high heat until oil reaches 350°F.
5. Add shrimp to flour mixture and toss to coat evenly, then dip in milk mixture, letting excess drip off, and return to flour and coat well. Add to hot oil. Fry 4 or 5 shrimp at a time until golden brown, about 2–3 minutes. Transfer to a paper towel–lined plate to drain. Repeat with remaining shrimp and batter. Serve immediately.

Shrimp Sizing

Shrimp sizing comes in ranges based on the average count per pound. Large shrimp, for example, are usually twenty-two to thirty shrimp per pound. The smallest designation is tiny (seventy-one to ninety shrimp per pound), and the biggest is extra colossal at ten per pound! Shrimp that are medium to extra large are best for grilling and frying.

RED ROBIN CRISPY ONION STRAWS

Typically Served With: Tavern Haystack Double Burger

Onion straws are great for dressing up a burger or sandwich, tossing into a salad, or serving with your favorite dips! These straws are typically served on the Red Robin Whiskey River BBQ Burger and the Tavern Haystack Double Burger, where they add savory flavor and a bit of crunch. They are easy to make, and the secret to their mild onion taste is a soak in buttermilk. This helps soften the flavor, leaving the sweet onion taste without any strong or overpowering onion flavors. They are best eaten fresh out of the oil, so make them just before serving. If you need to put them on hold, you can place them on a tray in a 170°F oven for about 20 minutes.

SERVES 4

1 large sweet onion, peeled and thinly sliced
1/2 cup low-fat buttermilk
3/4 cup all-purpose flour
1/2 teaspoon seasoning salt
2 cups vegetable oil

1. In a medium bowl, add onion and buttermilk. Toss to coat onion, then cover and let soak 30 minutes.
2. While onion soaks, combine flour and seasoning salt in a large resealable plastic bag and shake to combine.
3. Once soaked, drain excess buttermilk from onion. Place onion in bag with flour, seal, and shake well to coat.
4. Fill a 2-quart saucepan with oil over high heat and heat to 350°F.
5. Add onion and cook 2–3 minutes, turning occasionally, until golden brown and tender. Transfer to a paper towel–lined plate and cool 1 minute before serving. Enjoy warm.

More Ways to Use Onion Straws

Onion straws are a versatile side and garnish for all sorts of meals. They make a fun snack or appetizer with dip or can be piled onto burgers or chicken sandwiches, added to wraps for a bit of crunch, or used as a topping for steaks or grilled chicken or as a bed for fried or grilled seafood.

RED ROBIN CRISPY ONION STRAWS

TACO BELL NACHO FRIES

Typically Served With: Taco Bell Nacho Cheese Sauce

Nacho Fries, introduced in 2018, are known for their bold seasoning, addictive crunch, and elusiveness! Fans of the fries find it frustrating that they have been an on-again-off-again menu item for many years. Taco Bell has claimed that Nacho Fries are their most successful menu release in their history, and fans agree—they are delicious! Rumors come and go that the fries will join the permanent menu, and until they do you can enjoy them at home with this quick and easy recipe. Frozen fast-food-style French fries are the perfect base for the seasoning blend that is the signature of these fries. Enjoy them with some Taco Bell Nacho Cheese Sauce (Chapter 7) for dipping.

SERVES 8

1 teaspoon paprika
1/2 teaspoon onion powder
1/2 teaspoon chili powder
1/2 teaspoon sea salt
1/4 teaspoon garlic powder
1/4 teaspoon granulated sugar
Vegetable oil, for frying
1 pound frozen Ore-Ida Extra Crispy Fast Food Fries

1. In a small bowl, combine paprika, onion powder, chili powder, salt, garlic powder, and sugar. Mix well. Set aside.
2. Fill a deep fryer with oil per manufacturer directions and heat to 375°F. Or in a 5 1/2-quart Dutch oven, add enough oil to fill pot by 3 inches, leaving at least 3 inches of space at the top, and place over medium-high heat until oil reaches 350°F.
3. Working in batches, fry frozen fries 2–3 minutes until golden brown, transfer to a paper towel–lined plate, and sprinkle seasoning mix over fries. Serve immediately.

Frozen French Fries

Most fast-food restaurants, and many traditional sit-down restaurants, use frozen French fries. They make the process in the kitchen easier, they are uniform in cut and size, and frozen fries generally have a crispier exterior and fluffy interior. Freezing breaks up the flesh of the potatoes, which aids in fluffiness!

RECIPES BY RESTAURANT

Standard US/Metric Measurement Conversions

VOLUME CONVERSIONS

US Volume Measure	Metric Equivalent
⅛ teaspoon	0.5 milliliter
¼ teaspoon	1 milliliter
½ teaspoon	2 milliliters
1 teaspoon	5 milliliters
½ tablespoon	7 milliliters
1 tablespoon (3 teaspoons)	15 milliliters
2 tablespoons (1 fluid ounce)	30 milliliters
¼ cup (4 tablespoons)	60 milliliters
⅓ cup	90 milliliters
½ cup (4 fluid ounces)	125 milliliters
⅔ cup	160 milliliters
¾ cup (6 fluid ounces)	180 milliliters
1 cup (16 tablespoons)	250 milliliters
1 pint (2 cups)	500 milliliters
1 quart (4 cups)	1 liter (about)

WEIGHT CONVERSIONS

US Weight Measure	Metric Equivalent
½ ounce	15 grams
1 ounce	30 grams
2 ounces	60 grams
3 ounces	85 grams
¼ pound (4 ounces)	115 grams
½ pound (8 ounces)	225 grams
¾ pound (12 ounces)	340 grams
1 pound (16 ounces)	454 grams

OVEN TEMPERATURE CONVERSIONS

Degrees Fahrenheit	Degrees Celsius
200 degrees F	95 degrees C
250 degrees F	120 degrees C
275 degrees F	135 degrees C
300 degrees F	150 degrees C
325 degrees F	160 degrees C
350 degrees F	180 degrees C
375 degrees F	190 degrees C
400 degrees F	205 degrees C
425 degrees F	220 degrees C
450 degrees F	230 degrees C

BAKING PAN SIZES

American	Metric
8 × 1½ inch round baking pan	20 × 4 cm cake tin
9 × 1½ inch round baking pan	23 × 3.5 cm cake tin
11 × 7 × 1½ inch baking pan	28 × 18 × 4 cm baking tin
13 × 9 × 2 inch baking pan	30 × 20 × 5 cm baking tin
2 quart rectangular baking dish	30 × 20 × 3 cm baking tin
15 × 10 × 2 inch baking pan	30 × 25 × 2 cm baking tin (Swiss roll tin)
9 inch pie plate	22 × 4 or 23 × 4 cm pie plate
7 or 8 inch springform pan	18 or 20 cm springform or loose bottom cake tin
9 × 5 × 3 inch loaf pan	23 × 13 × 7 cm or 2 lb narrow loaf or pâté tin
1½ quart casserole	1.5 liter casserole
2 quart casserole	2 liter casserole

INDEX

T